House of Commons

Home Affairs and Work and Pensions Committees

Draft Corporate Manslaughter Bill

First Joint Report of Session 2005–06

Volume I: Report

First Report from the Home Affairs Committee of Session 2005–06

First Report from the Work and Pensions Committee of Session 2005–06

Report, together with formal minutes

*Ordered by The House of Commons
to be printed 12 December 2005*

HC 540-I
Published on 20 December 2005
by authority of the House of Commons
London: The Stationery Office Limited
£15.50

The Home Affairs and Work and Pensions Committees

The Home Affairs and Work and Pensions Committees are appointed by the House of Commons to examine the expenditure, administration, and policy of the Home Office and the Department for Work and Pensions.

Current membership

HOME AFFAIRS: Mr John Denham (Chairman)*, Mr Richard Benyon, Mr Jeremy Browne, Colin Burgon, Mr James Clappison, Mrs Ann Cryer, Mrs Janet Dean, Nick Harvey, Nick Herbert, Steve McCabe, Mr Shahid Malik, Gwyn Prosser, Mr Gary Streeter, Mr David Winnick.

WORK AND PENSIONS: Mr Terry Rooney (Chairman), Miss Anne Begg, Harry Cohen, Mr Philip Dunne, Mrs Natascha Engel, Michael Jabez Foster, Justine Greening, Mrs Joan Humble, Greg Mulholland, John Penrose, Jenny Willott.

*Mr John Denham, Chairman for this inquiry.

Powers

The Committees are departmental select committees, the powers of which are set out in House of Commons Standing Orders, principally in Standing Order No. 152. The powers of the Committees to work together and agree joint reports are set out in Standing Order No. 137A. These Standing Orders are available on the Internet via www.parliament.uk.

Publications

The Reports and evidence of the Committee are published by The Stationery Office by Order of the House. All publications of the Committee (including press notices) are on the Internet at www.parliament.uk/parliamentary_committees/home_affairs_committee/draft_corporate-manslaughter_bill.cfm.

Committee staff

The staff of the Draft Corporate Manslaughter Bill Sub-committees are Gosia McBride (Clerk), Manjit Gheera (Committee Legal Specialist), Francene Graham (Committee Assistant), and Jenny Pickard (Secretary).

Contacts

All correspondence should be addressed to the Clerk of the Home Affairs and Work and Pensions Draft Corporate Manslaughter Bill Sub-Committees, House of Commons, 7 Millbank, London SW1P 3JA. The telephone number for general enquiries is 020 7219 8387; the Committee's email address is homeaffcom@parliament.uk

Footnotes

In the footnotes of this Report, references to oral evidence are indicated by 'Q' followed by the question number. All oral evidence for this inquiry is printed in Volume III. References to written evidence are indicated by the page number as in 'Ev 12' (written evidence published in Volume is indicated as in 'Volume II, Ev 12, and evidence published in Volume III is indicated as in 'Volume III, Ev 12).

Contents

Summary

We are pleased that the Government has finally introduced a draft Corporate Manslaughter Bill. There is a strong need for a statutory offence that shifts the basis of liability for corporate manslaughter away from the requirement of identifying a 'directing mind' of a guilty company. This 'identification principle' has made prosecutions of large companies almost impossible under the current common law. It is now over eight years since the Government first announced it was going to consider such legislation and we would like to see an actual Bill introduced before the end of this parliamentary session 2005/06.

However, we are concerned that the current drafting of the Bill may not satisfy those who have previously felt so let down by the law. Although we welcome the removal of Crown immunity, we believe that some of the exemptions in the Bill are too broad. In particular we are concerned about the proposed exemption for deaths in police custody and prisons. In addition we recommend that the draft Bill should contain provision to prosecute an individual for contributing to the offence of corporate manslaughter and that the Government should have considered a wider package of corporate sanctions. We also believe that there should be no requirement to obtain the Director of Public Prosecution's consent before a private prosecution can be bought. The offence should also have wider territorial application than in the current draft Bill.

The proposed basis for liability in the draft Bill is more complex than it needs to be. The Government should remove the civil law concept of a duty of care in negligence from the Bill. It is surplus to requirements and adds unnecessary legal complication to the Bill. We also believe it is inappropriate to adopt a civil law concept as the basis for a criminal offence.

The restriction of management failure to that by senior managers is also problematic and has in effect reintroduced some of the problems of the 'identification principle'. We acknowledge the argument that the Law Commission's "management failure" test could cover failings within a company that occur at too low a level to be fairly associated with the company as a whole. We recommend that the Home Office should seek to address this specific concern without abandoning the Law Commission's general approach, which we support, of using 'management failure' as the basis for liability. We suggest that juries be assisted in their task by being required to consider whether there has been a serious breach of health and safety legislation and related guidance or other relevant legislation. In assessing this they could consider whether a corporate culture existed in the organisation that encouraged, tolerated or led to that management failure.

Introduction

The Committees' inquiry

1. The Government published its draft Corporate Manslaughter Bill on 23 March 2005.[1] Its consultation on the draft Bill ended on 17 June. The Home Affairs and Work and Pensions Committees had expressed an interest in this matter in the last Parliament and, on reappointment after the 2005 election, decided to examine the Government's proposals. In July 2005 we appointed draft Corporate Manslaughter Bill Sub-committees to meet concurrently "to consider and report on the Government's draft Corporate Manslaughter Bill".

2. On 20 July, the Sub-committees invited interested parties to submit written memoranda. We asked those who had already responded to the Home Office consultation for permission to use these responses as evidence, but also welcomed additional or updated memoranda from these respondents and others. We received over 150 submissions from a wide range of interested organisations and individuals.

3. The Government had expressed the hope that we would report to the House before Christmas and this timeframe restricted the amount of oral evidence we were able to take. We held six evidence sessions starting on 24 October 2005 and sought to hear from witnesses who represented a range of views articulated in written evidence. We made a particular effort to include individuals who had been bereaved by public disasters or deaths in the workplace, or organisations representing them. We regret that we were unable to hear from all of the organisations who contacted us during the course of the inquiry, requesting to be heard. However, we assure them and all those who submitted written evidence to our inquiry that we have fully taken into account all views expressed in written, as well as oral, evidence.

4. We took oral evidence from 29 organisations and individuals. They were: Disaster Action; the Simon Jones Memorial Campaign; Amicus; the Trades Union Congress; the Transport and General Workers' Union; the Centre for Corporate Accountability; the Law Reform Committee of the General Council of the Bar; the London Criminal Courts Solicitors' Association; Thompsons Solicitors; Professor Frank Wright; the Institution of Occupational Safety and Health; the Railway Forum; the Rail Safety and Standards Board; the Construction Confederation; the Royal Academy of Engineering; the Institute of Directors; EEF, the manufacturers' organisation; the Marchioness Contact Group; the Union of Construction Allied Trades and Technicians; the Confederation of British Industry; the Association of Principal Fire Officers; the Association of Chief Police Officers of England, Wales and Northern Ireland; the Police Federation of England and Wales; the Prison Reform Trust; JUSTICE; Lord Justice Judge; the Health and Safety Commission; the Health and Safety Executive; and the Parliamentary Under-Secretary of State at the Home Office, Fiona Mactaggart MP. The transcripts of all these sessions are printed in full in Volume III of the Report.

---

1 Home Office, *Corporate Manslaughter: The Government's Draft Bill for Reform*, Cm 6497, March 2005

5. We are grateful to all those who submitted written evidence or gave oral evidence to our inquiry. We would also like to express our thanks to our two Specialist Advisers: Professor Chris Clarkson, Professor and Dean of Law at the University of Leicester and Professor Celia Wells, Professor of Law at Cardiff University.

1 Background to the draft Bill

Why is the law being changed?

6. The last twenty years have seen thousands of people in the UK lose their lives in work-related or public disasters.[2] Some of these cases have been the subject of public inquiries which have been highly critical of the companies involved.[3] However, not one large company has yet been successfully prosecuted for manslaughter.

7. As the Home Office states in its introduction to the draft Bill, the failure to successfully prosecute a large company for manslaughter has resulted in "public concern that the law is not delivering justice".[4] It has particularly caused great frustration, distress and anger to those bereaved by these incidents. A mother who lost her daughter in the Marchioness riverboat tragedy[5] told us that the search for justice was "a horrendous path – something I would not bestow…on my worst enemy".[6]

8. We have taken the view throughout this report that the key issue to consider when examining the proposals is whether they satisfy those who have previously felt so let down by the law.

The identification principle

9. Under the current common law, a company can in theory be prosecuted for gross negligence manslaughter. However, in practice it is almost impossible successfully to prosecute a large company for the offence.

10. The main difficulty with the common law offence arises from the "identification principle". This means that a company can only be convicted of manslaughter if a person, who can be identified as the "directing mind" of the company, is individually guilty of the gross negligence which resulted in the death in question. A "directing mind" is an individual in the company who is sufficiently senior to be "identified as the embodiment of the company itself".[7] Unless it can be shown that this very senior director or manager is guilty of gross negligence manslaughter, the prosecution of the company will fail.

11. It has proved very difficult to identify a "directing mind" in all but the smallest of companies. Complex management structures and the delegation of responsibilities in

---

2 Between 1992 and 2005, 3425 workers were killed. Last year alone, 220 workers and 361 members of the public were killed. Health and Safety Commission and National Statistics, *Health and safety statistics 2004/05*, p 5-6

3 After the 1987 Herald of Free Enterprise ferry disaster, in which 150 passengers and 38 crew lost their lives, Lord Justice Sheen published a report which found that from "top to bottom the body corporate was infected with the disease of sloppiness". (Mr Justice Sheen, `1987 mv Herald of Free Enterprise` (formal investigation). London: HMSO, Report of Court No 8074) In an inquiry into the 1988 Piper Alpha fire, in which 167 workers lost their lives, Lord Cullen found that there were "significant flaws in Occidental's management of safety". (The Hon Lord Cullen. `The Public Inquiry into the Piper Alfa Disaster` London: HMSO, 1990)

4 Home Office, *Corporate Manslaughter: The Government's Draft Bill for Reform*, Cm 6497, March 2005, p 8

5 On 20 August 1989, a dredger crashed into the Marchioness pleasure cruiser which was filled with people at a party. Over 50 people lost their lives.

6 Volume III, Q 298 [Mrs Dallaglio]

7 R v HM Coroner for East Kent, ex p Spooner (1989) 88 CR App R 10, 16 per Bingham LJ

larger companies make it less likely that an individual can be identified as embodying a company in his or her actions or decisions. Of the (34) work-related manslaughter prosecutions brought since 1992, only seven have succeeded. All seven were against small companies or sole traders.

A new basis for liability

12. The Government's draft Bill aims to "enable more prosecutions to proceed by tackling …the difficulties created by the identification principle". The new proposals change the basis of liability from the requirement of identifying a "directing mind" of a company that is guilty of gross negligence manslaughter, to a test that considers the adequacy of the way in which an organisation's activities are managed or organised by its senior managers.[8]

13. The majority of our witnesses, including victims' groups, unions and industry, welcomed the Government's decision to change the basis of liability for corporate manslaughter.[9] For example, the Trades Union Congress submitted:

> "The TUC has, for many years been aware of the failings within the existing law and believes that this change is necessary if corporate responsibility on health and safety is to be improved, and the relatives of those killed as a result of corporate failings are to see justice done".[10]

The Federation of Master Builders believed it would help to:

> "even the playing field in relation to the clearly uneven way in which justice is currently applied to those who operate with scant regard for human life".[11]

14. However, some of those who submitted evidence to the inquiry did not believe that a new statutory offence was necessary. A small number believed that the combination of the common law offence and health and safety offences was a sufficient deterrent[12] and that a statutory offence would create a blame culture where lessons could not be learned.[13] Others argued that courts simply needed to make full use of the sanctions already available under existing health and safety legislation (see "Sanctions" Chapter 12).[14] Professor G R Sullivan, Professor in the Department of Law at Durham University, suggested that creating an aggravated version of health and safety offences with increased penalties, whenever a failure on the part of the company or organisation to provide a reasonably practicable safe system of work constituted a cause of death, might be a preferable alternative.[15]

---

8 Home Office, *Corporate Manslaughter: The Government's Draft Bill for Reform*, Cm 6497, March 2005, p 8-9

9 Volume II, Ev 1, 3, 12, 16, 18, 30, 38, 43, 44, 54, 58, 59, 65, 69, 79, 85, 87, 110, 112, 132, 135, 148, 152, 192 (Health and Safety Commission), 192 (Communication Workers" Union), 202, 205, 209 (Association of British Insurers), 209 (Institute of Electrical Engineers), 211, 214, 226, 227, 228, 231, 232, 237, 238, 270, 275, 278, 282, 283, 296, 297, 298, 299, 301,305, 309, 316 and 317

10 Volume II, Ev 16

11 Volume II, Ev 1

12 Volume II, Ev 150 and 277

13 Volume II, Ev 69, 130, 150 and 303

14 Volume II, Ev 222

15 Volume II, Ev 33

15. Notwithstanding these views, we believe that there is public demand for an offence that lies outside the health and safety regulatory scheme. The evidence we received appeared to show that those bereaved placed a high value on a successful prosecution for a *serious* criminal offence. For example, the mother of a young person killed in the workplace told the Sub-committees:

> "a successful prosecution brings into the public domain all the failings that led to a preventable death and, very importantly, it shows that this country values all human life and is prepared to punish those who are negligent or indifferent to the lives of workers. It would make people with the real power in an organisation accept responsibility for what they have done. Most importantly, it allows lessons to be learned from mistakes and acts as a spur to other employers to rectify similar problems. Also, it gives the only consolation available to the bereaved family, that their son, daughter, husband or wife has not died in vain but that by their loss the annual carnage involved in work-related incidents in Britain will cease".[16]

16. **We welcome the Government's proposal to introduce a statutory offence of corporate manslaughter.**

History of the current proposals

The Law Commission's proposals

17. The Government's proposals in the draft Bill have had a long gestation. The first step towards changing the existing law was taken in 1994, when the Law Commission published a consultation paper setting out its provisional proposals for reforming the law on involuntary manslaughter.[17] In light of responses to its consultation, the Commission presented a report in 1996 which made a number of recommendations.[18] These included:

- abolishing the offence of involuntary manslaughter;

- replacing it by two new offences: "reckless killing" and "killing by gross carelessness"; and

- creating a special offence of "corporate killing".[19]

18. The Commission recommended that for the new corporate offence a death should be regarded as having been caused by the conduct of an organisation "if it is caused by a failure in the way in which the corporation's activities are managed or organised to ensure the health and safety of persons employed in or affected by those activities". Corporate killing was broadly to correspond to the suggested individual offence of killing by gross carelessness. The Commission recommended that the corporate offence, like the suggested new individual offence, should be committed only when the organisation's conduct in

16 Volume III, Q 3 [Anne Jones]

17 Law Commission, *Criminal Law: Involuntary Manslaughter Consultation Paper No 135*, 1994

18 Law Commission, *Legislating the Criminal code: Involuntary Manslaughter: Item 11 of the Sixth Programme of Law Reform: Criminal Law: Report No 237*, HC (1995-96) 171

19 Law Commission, HC (1995-96) 171, pp 127-131

causing the death fell far below what could reasonably be expected of the organisation in the circumstances.[20]

19. The Commission also recommended that the offence should be capable of commission by any corporation, however and wherever incorporated (so including abroad), other than a corporation sole, but that it should not be capable of commission by unincorporated bodies or by an individual, even as a second party. Other recommendations included that there should be liability for the corporate offence only if the injury that resulted in death occurred in a place over which the English courts would have had jurisdiction if the offence had been committed by a non-British subject; that there should be no requirement of consent for the bringing of private prosecutions for the corporate offence; and that on conviction the court should have power to give remedial orders.[21]

20. Between 1997 and 2000, the Government gave a series of commitments to look into the Law Commission's proposals (see 'Delays and timing' paras 37 to 49).

21. In February 2000, the Court of Appeal gave an opinion on the identification principle. This followed the ruling in June 1999 that Great Western Trains could only be convicted for corporate manslaughter in the Southall rail crash[22] via the guilt of a human being with whom it might be identified. The Court of Appeal's opinion ruled that in the present state of the common law, the identification principle remained the only basis for corporate liability for gross negligent manslaughter. The opinion referred to the Law Commission's recommendations, but did not think it appropriate for the Court to push the law in this direction, arguing that this was "a matter for Parliament, not the courts".[23]

22. In April 2000, Mr Andrew Dismore MP introduced a Ten Minute Rule Bill to create a new criminal offence of corporate killing.[24] However, the Bill was not supported by the Government and was unable to proceed.

The Government's 2000 Consultation Paper

23. In May 2000, the Government published a consultation document based on the Law Commission's recommendations.[25] The document went further than the proposals in some respects. It suggested that:

- all forms of undertaking, including partnerships, schools, unincorporated charities and small businesses, should be liable for the offence;[26]

- any individual who could be shown to have had some influence on, or responsibility for, the circumstances in which a management failure falling far below what could

---

20 Law Commission, HC (1995-96) 171, pp 128-129

21 Law Commission, HC (1995-96) 171, pp 129-130

22 In September 1997, a high speed train from Swansea collided into a freight train at Southall. Seven people were killed and over 150 injured.

23 Attorney-General's Reference 2/99, 15 February 2000, Lord Justice Rose

24 Corporate Homicide Bill [Bill 114 (1999/2000)]

25 Home Office, *Reforming the Law on Involuntary Manslaughter: The Government's Proposals*, May 2000

26 Home Office, May 2000, para 3.5.1

reasonably be expected was a cause of a person's death should be subject to a disqualification from acting in a management role in any undertaking carrying on a business or activity in Great Britain;[27]

- the health and safety enforcing authorities and possibly other enforcement agencies should investigate and prosecute the new offences, in addition to the police and Crown Prosecution Service; [28] and that

- it should also be possible to take action against parent or other group companies if it could be shown that their own management failures were a cause of the death concerned.[29]

24. The Government also invited views on whether it would be right in principle that officers of undertakings who contributed to the management failure resulting in death, should be liable to a penalty of imprisonment in separate criminal proceedings;[30] on the application of Crown immunity to the offence of corporate killing;[31] and on whether it would ever be appropriate to permit the prosecuting authority to institute proceedings to freeze company assets before criminal proceedings started in order to prevent assets being transferred to evade fines or compensation orders.[32]

25. There were over 150 responses to the Home Office consultation from unions, industry, the public sector and members of the public. These displayed strong support for reform of the existing law; support for wide application of the offence to cover all undertakings, including the removal of Crown immunity; divided views on individual liability and very mixed opinions on the issue of investigation and prosecution. A number of witnesses questioned the construction of the proposed offence and suggested other ways of addressing the shortcomings in current law, including more vigorous enforcement of health and safety legislation.[33]

The Government's draft Bill

26. The Government's draft Bill was finally published on 23 March 2005. The proposals in the draft Bill differ from the proposals in the Government's 2000 consultation document and the Law Commission's recommendations in certain respects (including changing the title of the offence from "corporate *killing*" to "corporate *manslaughter*").

27. The proposals in the draft Bill use the Law Commission's suggestion that the new offence should be based on failures in the way an organisation's activities were managed or organised. However, they add a further requirement which did not appear in either the

---

27 Home Office, May 2000, para 3.4.9

28 Home Office, May 2000, para 3.3.5

29 Home Office, May 2000, para 3.4.6

30 Home Office, May 2000, para 3.4.13

31 Home Office, May 2000, para 3.2.8

32 Home Office, May 2000, para 3.4.16

33 Home Office, *Corporate Manslaughter: A Summary of Responses to the Home Office's Consultation in 2000*

Law Commission proposals or the Government's previous consultation document. This requirement is that management failings are by an organisation's *senior managers.*

28. The Law Commission proposed that a new offence be based on a failure to ensure the health and safety of employees or members of the public. However, it did not define the relationship between this and duties imposed by health and safety legislation and duties imposed under the common law to take reasonable care for the safety of others.[34]

29. The Government's draft Bill defines a relevant duty of care as that owed under the law of negligence by an organisation:

- as employer or occupier of land, or

- when supplying goods or services or when engaged in other commercial activities (for example, in mining or fishing)

other than when carrying out exclusively public functions - that is activities performed by the Government under the prerogative or those that are a type of activity (whether carried out by a private or public sector body) that requires a statutory or prerogative basis. The Bill also exempts decisions involving matters of public policy.

30. The draft Bill adopts the Law Commission's proposal to define gross failure in terms of conduct that falls far below what can reasonably be expected in the circumstances. However, it also provides a range of factors for juries to consider when assessing an organisation's culpability, including failure to comply with health and safety legislation and guidance, and whether or not its senior managers were aware, or ought to have been aware, of the breach and whether they had any intention to profit from the breach.

31. The draft Bill applies the new offence to corporations but not to unincorporated bodies. It also removes Crown immunity although it includes a number of exemptions. Under the Bill, a parent company (as well as any subsidiary) would be liable to prosecution where it owed a duty of care to the victim in respect of any of the activities covered by the offence and a gross management failure by its senior managers caused death.

32. The draft Bill does not propose to create new sanctions for individuals. It also explicitly excludes the possibility of convicting individuals for being a secondary party to the offence.[35]

33. Unlike the Law Commission's draft Bill, the Home Office's proposed draft Bill does not include a separate provision to deal with the issue of establishing that a management failure can cause death even when an intervening act may appear to have broken the chain of causation.[36]

34. The draft Bill proposes that the current responsibilities of the police to investigate and the Crown Prosecution Service to prosecute corporate manslaughter will not change.

---

34 Law Commission, *Legislating the Criminal code: Involuntary Manslaughter: Item 11 of the Sixth Programme of Law Reform: Criminal Law: Report No 237,* HC (1995-96) 171,

35 Home Office, *Corporate Manslaughter: The Government's Draft Bill for Reform,* Cm 6497, March 2005, para 47

36 *Draft Corporate Manslaughter Bill,* paras 50-51

35. Unlike the Government's 2000 consultation paper, the draft Bill requires the consent of the Director of Public Prosecutions before private proceedings in respect of the new offence can be instituted.

36. A table comparing and contrasting the proposals suggested by the Law Commission, the proposals in the Government's 2000 Consultation Paper and those in the draft Corporate Manslaughter Bill can be found at Annex 1.

Delays and timing

37. Many witnesses expressed frustration that the publication of the draft Bill had been far later than they expected.[37] The GMB, for example, felt it had taken "an inexcusably long time to emerge".[38] Since we are now hearing media reports that the Cabinet has decided to shelve the Corporate Manslaughter Bill,[39] we feel it is important to remind the Government of its repeated commitments over the last eight years to act on this issue.

38. In October 1997, a month after the Southall rail crash, the then Home Secretary, the Rt Hon Jack Straw MP, told the Labour party conference: "Many countries have laws which provide for the conviction of company directors where it's claimed that dreadful negligence by the company as a whole has meant people have died". He added that there was a "strong argument for considering in detail" the introduction of such laws in the UK.[40]

39. The Home Office's consultation paper did not appear until May 2000.

40. On 6 December 2000, the Government gave a loosely worded commitment in the Queen's Speech promising that a bill would be drafted that would "provide for safer travel on the railways, in the air, at sea and on the roads, and will take forward proposals for revitalising health and safety at work".[41]

41. In 2001 the Labour Party manifesto stated that "law reform is necessary to make provisions against corporate manslaughter".[42]

42. On 14 March 2002 the then Parliamentary Under-Secretary of State for Transport, Local Government and the Regions, Dr Alan Whitehead MP, confirmed that a bill on corporate killing would be introduced when time permitted.[43] In September 2002, the Government again raised hopes that the draft Bill would be published shortly by distributing an impact assessment questionnaire to the private sector, including industries with a high injury rate over the last five years, with a deadline of 1 November 2002 for

37 Volume II, Ev 6, 18, 54, 108, 110, 193, 215-216, 253, 306, and 316

38 Volume II, Ev 59

39 "The unions are also likely to be angered by a cabinet decision last week to shelve a proposed corporate manslaughter bill." *The Sunday Times*, 27 November 2005, p1

40 *The Financial Times*, 3 October 1997

41 HC Deb, 6 Dec 2000, col 4

42 Labour Party, *Ambitions for Britain: Labour's manifesto 2001*, p 32

43 HC Deb, 14 March 2002, col 358WH

responses.[44] However, the Government failed to publish the draft Bill in the parliamentary session 2002-03.

43. On 21 May 2003 the Home Office issued a press release promising that "a timetable for legislation and further details would be announced in the autumn", thus further postponing any real action.[45]

44. The next twelve months saw another series of commitments that draft legislation would soon be published. On 2 December 2003, the then Home Secretary, Rt Hon David Blunkett MP, promised to publish a draft bill "very shortly".[46] On 29 April 2004, the Minister for the Criminal Justice System and Offender Management, Baroness Patricia Scotland QC, in a speech at the Centre for Corporate Accountability's conference on corporate killing, promised that a draft Bill would be published before the end of the parliamentary session 2003-04.[47]

45. On 23 July 2004, in a report into the work of the Health and Safety Commission and Executive, the Work and Pensions Committee, expressed concern "at the length of time it is taking the Government to resolve any outstanding issues concerning reforms of the law on corporate killing" and recommended that the Government publish its draft Bill by 1 December 2004.[48] In its response to that report, the Government said it still intended to publish a draft Bill that autumn.[49]

46. The Prime Minister reiterated this commitment at a speech to the Trades Union Congress conference on 13 September 2004.[50] Shortly afterwards, on 29 September 2004, the then Home Secretary, Rt Hon David Blunkett MP, told the Labour Party conference that he was "confirming this afternoon that we will publish this autumn the draft bill on corporate killing that has been awaited for so long".[51]

47. Autumn, and parliamentary session 2003-04 came and went. In the Queen's Speech on 23 November 2004, the Government again promised that a draft bill would be published.

48. The draft Bill was finally published on 23 March 2005. The Queen's Speech following the General Election on 17 May 2005 restated the Government's intention to introduce an offence of corporate manslaughter. In oral evidence, the Parliamentary Under-Secretary of State at the Home Office, Fiona Mactaggart MP, told us that the Government would introduce the actual Bill " as soon as Parliamentary time allows".[52]

44 Home Office, *Corporate Manslaughter: A Regulatory Impact Assessment of the Government's Draft Bill*, para 12

45 "Government to tighten laws on corporate killing", Home Office press release 142/2003, 21 May 2003

46 HC Deb, 2 December 2003, col 385

47 www.corporateaccountability.org

48 Work and Pensions Committee, Fourth Report of Session 2003-04, *The Work of the Health and Safety Commission and Executive*, HC 456-I, para 53

49 Work and Pensions Committee, Third Special Report of Session 2003-04, *Government Response to the Committee's Fourth Report into the Work of the Health and Safety Commission and Executive*, HC 1137, p 4

50 Full text of speech available at www.politics.guardian.co.uk .

51 Full text of speech available at www.labour.org.uk .

52 Volume III, Q 600

49. We are concerned at the length of time it has taken the Government to introduce a draft Bill since it first promised legislation on corporate manslaughter. We believe there should be no further unnecessary delay. We urge the Government to introduce the Bill, including our recommended changes, by the end of the present parliamentary session, making provision for carry-over if necessary.

2 Application of the offence

50. The new offence of corporate manslaughter will apply to "organisations". An organisation is defined in clause 1(2) of the draft Bill as:

(a) "a corporation"; or

(b) "a government department or other body listed in the Schedule" (see para 63 below).

51. Clause 7 of the draft Bill removes Crown immunity for the offence so that, in principle, Crown bodies which are either corporations or are one of the government departments listed in the Schedule to the draft Bill, can be prosecuted for an offence of corporate manslaughter (removal of Crown immunity is discussed further in Chapter 10). We discuss each limb of this definition in turn below. We then consider the particular case of police forces.

Corporations

52. A corporation is defined in the draft Bill as including any body corporate, wherever incorporated, except a corporation sole.[53] Partnerships, sole traders, and other unincorporated bodies, such as certain clubs and associations, are therefore excluded from the scope of the offence.

53. The application of the offence to corporations follows the original recommendation of the Law Commission (see para 19) that the offence of corporate killing should be capable of commission by any corporation (other than a corporation sole) but that it should not extend to unincorporated bodies. The Law Commission's report stated:

> "It would clearly be wrong to extend the offence to *all* unincorporated bodies, because there are many such bodies (for example a partnership of two individuals employing no-one) that would be unfairly disadvantaged by being charged with the corporate offence [...] Any extension of the offence beyond incorporated bodies would therefore raise intractable problems as to the *kinds* of unincorporated body that ought not to be included".[54]

54. The application of the draft Bill to corporate bodies does, however, differ from the position the Government took in 2000 when it had declared that it did not wish "to create artificial barriers between incorporated and non-incorporated bodies".[55] In the introduction to the draft Bill the Home Office has justified its new position on the basis that unincorporated associations do not have a distinct legal personality to which liability can be assigned:

---

53 Clause 5

54 Law Commission, *Legislating the Criminal code: Involuntary Manslaughter: Item 11 of the Sixth Programme of Law Reform: Criminal Law: Report No 237,* HC (1995-96), para 8.55

55 Home Office, *Reforming the Law on Involuntary Manslaughter: The Government's Proposals,* May 2000, para 3.5.1

"This is not simply a legal technicality but means that they do not exist as a legal person in the way that corporations do. As such, they cannot currently be prosecuted for gross negligence manslaughter, although individual members might".[56]

55. Some of our witnesses agreed with the decision to limit the offence to bodies corporate.[57] The President of the Queen's Bench Division, Lord Justice Judge, warned that including unincorporated associations within the scope of the offence in the draft Bill could "produce potentially serious miscarriages of justice" where small partnerships were being prosecuted:

"Let us take two men, two people who run a business. The example that was drawn to my attention is running a gas fitting system. Partner A is negligent, something goes wrong, the elderly lady in the house has a cold and does not smell the gas and she dies. Partner B is not there at all; Partner B is working at another house doing a job perfectly well and has no idea what Partner A is up to. You could end up in that partnership with a very heavy fine, rightly imposed for the negligence of A, which has very serious effects on Partner B".[58]

56. A significant number of witnesses, however, criticised the Government's decision and called for the offence to be extended to all undertakings,[59] and in particular to all employing organisations.[60] The Transport and General Workers Union submitted that:

"Any organisation - regardless of whether it is a private company, an unincorporated body or a Crown body - can cause risk to its workers and to members of the public. Therefore, if a corporate manslaughter law is to be effective then it must apply to every employing organisation, including unincorporated bodies and all Crown bodies".[61]

57. Others shared this opinion but acknowledged the difficulties in extending the scope of the offence to all unincorporated bodies.[62] Hugh Robertson from the Trades Union Congress argued:

"We would like to see as broad a definition as possible but we do recognise the difficulties in drafting legislation that covers every single opportunity… Rather than making sure that every single individual, two-person, one-person, organisation is covered, the focus is to ensure that all large employers…are covered, [as] the problem is primarily large, unincorporated bodies".[63]

58. The Parliamentary Under-Secretary of State at the Home Office responded to this point in questioning by stating:

---

56 Home Office, *Corporate Manslaughter: The Government's Draft Bill for Reform*, Cm 6497, March 2005, para 41

57 See for example Volume II, Ev 113 and 119, and Volume III, Q 71 [Mr Donnellan].

58 Volume III, Q 494

59 See, for example, Volume III, Q 277 [Mr Day] and Volume II, Ev 43 and 49.

60 For example, Volume II, Ev 6, 24, 84, 103, and 133.

61 Volume II, Ev 24

62 See, for example, Volume III, Q 71 [Mr Donnellan].

63 Volume III, Q 31

> "You could prosecute them [unincorporated bodies] in terms of their health and safety liabilities as an employer, which is the most likely occasion on which it might arise, but actually I do not think you could give them a corporate responsibility if they are not a corporation…One of our difficulties is that we have to draw a line somewhere and the easiest way to draw a line is where there actually is a corporate entity rather than trying to turn something which is not an entity into an entity".[64]

59. However, a selection of named unincorporated bodies are already included within the scope of the offence by virtue of being listed in the Schedule to the draft Bill. In Canada the federal criminal law has recently been altered to impose criminal liability on a wider range of "organisations" than under the draft Bill. The Canadian definition includes "a public body, body corporate, society, company, firm, partnership, trade union or municipality".[65]

60. The Home Office has also argued that there does not appear to be a problem in practice with the inability to prosecute unincorporated bodies under the common law:

> "…[the issue is] whether the law should be extended to apply to a new range of organisations. We have not established that the inability to bring a prosecution against an unincorporated body *itself* for manslaughter, as opposed to any of its members individually, creates a problem in practice".[66]

61. The Health and Safety at Work etc. Act 1974 applies to both incorporated and unincorporated bodies. However, the Health and Safety Commission was unfortunately unable to give us any information about how many unincorporated associations have been prosecuted for health and safety offences.[67]

62. **As the Government's proposals stand, it will be possible to prosecute corporations under the provisions in the draft Bill, and individuals running smaller unincorporated bodies will be able to be prosecuted under the common law individual offence of gross negligence manslaughter. However, a gap in the law will remain for large unincorporated bodies such as big partnerships of accounting and law firms. We are concerned that such major organisations will be outside the scope of the Bill and would recommend that the Government look at a way in which they could be brought within its scope. We urge the Government to provide us with statistics in order to support its claim that the inability to prosecute large unincorporated bodies does not cause problems in practice. We would be particularly interested in seeing statistics detailing how many large unincorporated bodies have been prosecuted and convicted of health and safety offences.**

Schedule of government departments or other bodies

63. In addition to the Crown bodies that are already covered by the draft Bill by virtue of being corporations, the Schedule to the draft Bill sets out a list of government departments and other bodies to which the offence will also extend. The Government has stated that:

---

64 Volume III, Q 571 and Q 573 (Fiona Mactaggart MP)

65 Criminal Code, Chapter C-46, Section 2

66 Home Office, *Corporate Manslaughter: The Government's Draft Bill for Reform*, Cm 6497, March 2005, para 43

67 Volume III, Q 535 [Mr Rees]

"Further work is required to develop this list, particularly to consider the position of executive agencies and other bodies that come under the ambit of Departments".[68]

64. A number of witnesses thought that the Schedule was too limited in scope. The then Lord Chief Justice Woolf, for example, described it as "remarkably short".[69] Witnesses suggested adding bodies to the Schedule including Parliament,[70] the National Assembly for Wales,[71] the Crown Estates,[72] the Food Standards Agency[73] and the Health and Safety Executive.[74] The manufacturers' organisation, EEF, criticised the principle of providing an exhaustive list by means of a Schedule. It argued that a list should be for "indicative purposes only and not exhaustive, as there are regular reorganisations of such bodies and any exhaustive list would quickly become out of date".[75]

65. **We welcome the certainty provided by an exhaustive list of government departments and other bodies and believe that the alternative, providing a statutory definition, could prove very difficult if not impossible to achieve. We agree with the Home Office that the draft Schedule needs "further work" to ensure that a number of other bodies, including a range of executive agencies, are included. It should also be reviewed by the Home Office on an ongoing basis, and formally every six months to ensure it is up to date. We think it might also be useful to extend clause 7 to ensure that bodies which are successors to bodies included in the Schedule are treated as "organisations" to which the offence applies.**

66. We also point out that if the Government were to decide to amend the definition of "organisation" to include unincorporated bodies there might be no need to include a Schedule listing Government departments and other bodies as, depending on the way such a wider definition was worded, such bodies might already fall within the scope of the offence.

67. The draft Bill proposes to delegate to the Home Secretary the power to amend the Schedule by secondary legislation.[76] This power would be subject to the negative resolution procedure. It would accordingly be possible for the Home Secretary to take bodies into and out of the scope of the offence without an explicit decision by Parliament to approve such changes, subject only to the possibility that Parliament could annul any order made by him. This power has been criticised by some witnesses as excessive.[77] An alternative would be for the power to be subject to the affirmative procedure, under which Parliament would have to make an active decision to agree to an amendment to the Schedule proposed by the Secretary of State. We prefer this option. **We recommend that the Home Secretary's**

---

68 *Draft Corporate Manslaughter Bill*, para 39

69 Volume II, Ev 109

70 Volume II, Ev 8 and 24

71 Volume II, Ev 31

72 Volume II, Ev 59

73 Volume II, Ev 79

74 Volume II, Ev 79

75 Volume II, Ev 230

76 Clause 1(3)

77 Volume II, Ev 32 and 86

delegated power to amend the Schedule should be subject to the affirmative resolution procedure rather than the negative resolution procedure.

Police forces

68. The proposed offence of corporate manslaughter will apply to police *authorities*, as they are incorporated bodies, but since police *forces* are not incorporated and are not listed in the Schedule, they would not be covered. However, in the introduction to the draft Bill, the Government stated:

> "We do not consider that, in principle, police forces should be outside the scope of the offence and our intention is that legislation should in due course extend to them. We are currently considering how best to achieve this, given their particular legal status".[78]

69. The Association of Chief Police Officers agreed with the Government that the police, like the Crown, should not be exempt from prosecution where they "are in no different position to other employers and organisations".[79] We discuss the exemption for police operational activities in Chapter 10.

70. In oral evidence to the Sub-committees, the Parliamentary Under-Secretary for State at the Home Office, Fiona Mactaggart MP, confirmed that the Government would ensure police forces were included when the Bill was published but that the mechanism by which this would be done had not yet been finalised.[80]

71. **It is appropriate that police forces as well as police authorities should be subject to the proposed new offence. We welcome the Government's assurances that the Bill when introduced will contain such provision.**

78 *Draft Corporate Manslaughter Bill*, para 44

79 Volume II, Ev 323

80 Volume III, Q 574

3 Death

72. Clause 1(1)(a) of the draft Bill proposes that an offence would be committed where:

- there is a **death** ;

- this is **caused** by the way an organisation's activities are **managed or organised** by its **senior managers;**

- the organisation owes a **relevant duty of care** to the deceased; AND

- the management failure constitutes a **gross breach** of the relevant duty of care.

73. We consider each of the terms highlighted in the chapters below. This chapter considers the issue of death.

Workers and the public

74. The offence not only covers the deaths of workers but also include deaths of members of the public when they were owed a relevant duty of care by the organisation (see Chapter 5 for further discussion of a relevant duty of care). Passenger deaths in major transport accidents are therefore included. We note that this differs from the equivalent statutory provision in another jurisdiction – the Australian Capital Territory (see para 125) – which frames the offence entirely in terms of employers killing workers.[81] A number of organisations witnesses supported the Government's broader approach.[82] **We welcome the Government's proposal that the offence not be limited only to the deaths of workers.**

Serious injuries

75. The offence only applies in the case of death and not, for example, serious injuries caused by senior management failures. According to the Health and Safety Commission, while there were 220 fatal injuries to workers in 2004/05, 30,213 employees sustained major injuries.[83]

76. Some witnesses felt that the failure to extend the application of the new offence to cover serious injuries would diminish its deterrent effect.[84] The Occupational and Environmental Health Research Group at the University of Stirling argued that "it may be sending out a confusing message to say that we will criminalize serious offences that result in death and not those that don't".[85] The Communication Workers' Union pointed out that the corporate liability provisions in Canada apply to both manslaughter and injury.[86]

---

81 Crimes Act 1900 (amended by Australian Capital Territory Crimes (Industrial Manslaughter) Amendment Act 2003)

82 Volume II, Ev 17, 30 and 298

83 National Statistics and Health and Safety Commission, *Health and safety statistics 2004/05,* p 5-6

84 Volume III, Q 27 [Mr Griffiths]

85 Volume II, Ev 11

86 Volume II, Ev 257

77. Other witnesses added that it was illogical that in the same circumstances a company could be liable for the offence if an incident resulted in death, and yet escape liability if the individual involved happened to be saved from death due to the quick actions of emergency services or sheer luck.[87] Rebecca Huxley-Binns and Michael Jefferson, from Nottingham and Sheffield Law Schools respectively, argued:

> "if two workers suffer from a splash of hot metal at a steel foundry occasioned by a gross breach by a senior manager as defined in the bill…then…it is absurd that if one died the company would be convicted of the proposed offence, but the company would not be liable for the other worker's serious injury - who was saved…only by the rapid intervention of a skilled paramedic".[88]

78. Representatives from the construction industry accepted in oral evidence to the Sub-committees that there was an argument for extending the offence.[89] Although the Chairman of the Construction Confederation warned against trying to do too much in one Bill, he appeared to support the eventual extension of the offence:

> "we are big believers in not being able to run before you can walk…, but surely in time it must be extended".[90]

79. However, other witnesses felt that incidents other than death were best handled by existing health and safety legislation.[91] We note that the Canadian Criminal Code also has an *individual* offence of causing injury by criminal negligence, whereas in England and Wales only manslaughter (and deaths caused by dangerous driving) are based on a negligence standard. Thus extending this draft Bill to injuries would be to create a corporate offence where there is no equivalent individual offence, which is arguably inequitable.

80. The Scottish Expert Group on Culpable Homicide, set up to report to Scottish ministers on the law on corporate liability for culpable homicide in Scotland, was divided on the issue, with some members feeling that any offence introduced should be extended to cover serious injuries, but others considering that this "could lead to dilution of the corporate killing offence and could potentially over-stretch investigation and enforcement resources".[92] (The findings of the Scottish Expert Group are discussed in Chapter 11).

81. **We believe that organisations should be punished where their failings cause serious injury but are not convinced that gross negligence resulting in serious injury needs to be brought within the scope of the draft Bill. If the draft Bill was amended in this way, it might lose its current clear focus on manslaughter, and the ensuing controversy and drafting difficulties might further delay the introduction of the actual Bill. We would, however, urge the Government to consider the possibility of using the Corporate**

87 Volume II, Ev 11, 55, 263 and 255

88 Volume II, Ev 55

89 Volume III, Q 211 [Mr Smith] and Q 222 [Mr Commins]

90 Volume III, Q 222

91 Volume II, Ev 261 and Volume III, Q 519 [Lord Justice Judge]

92 Scottish Executive, *Corporate Homicide: Expert Group Report*, November 2005, p 16

Manslaughter Act as a template for introducing further criminal offences, such as an offence of corporate grievous bodily harm, in due course.

Fatal damage to health

82. A number of witnesses were concerned that the offence, as currently proposed, would only capture deaths which are due to one-off incidents.[93] The Royal Society for the Prevention of Accidents, for example, believed that if the draft Bill were enacted in its present form, it would be very difficult to show causation through management failure where fatal damage to health was caused by sustained exposure to harmful agents or by the contraction of diseases with long latency.[94]

83. However, other witnesses argued that any difficulties in achieving successful prosecutions in such cases would not arise from the drafting of the legislation, but from a lack of resources for investigating and gathering evidence. The Occupational and Environmental Health Research Group at the University of Stirling, for example, submitted:

> "In the UK at the moment there remains a woeful lack of enforcement for offences that cause deaths and diseases following exposure to harmful substances (such as the exposure of workers to asbestos or chemicals). Across the UK, only 1% of deaths resulting from occupational exposures, as opposed to sudden deaths from injuries, are currently prosecuted as offences. Any new law on corporate killing will by definition, cover many of those deaths caused by exposure to harmful substances. This is not so much a substantive issue of law, but an issue relating to the gathering of evidence and of the rules and procedures used in investigations. The government should immediately review those aspects of evidence gathering and investigation used by the police and the HSE following deaths related to occupational health causes. Those aspects of the process are also resource intensive and we would urge the government to provide resources immediately to reverse the unacceptable shortfall in occupational health related prosecutions".[95]

84. **We are satisfied that the Bill as currently drafted covers long-term fatal damage to health as well as deaths caused by immediate injury. However, we would urge the Government to ensure that sufficient resources are available and appropriate procedures in place to make certain that in practice prosecutions are brought for deaths related to occupational health causes.**

Corporate "killing"

85. Some witnesses also criticised the title of the proposed offence. Rebecca Huxley-Binns and Michael Jefferson, of Nottingham and Sheffield Law Schools respectively, for example,

---

93 Volume II, Ev 67

94 Volume II, Ev 44

95 Volume II, Ev 11

argued that manslaughter was an "outdated" term "which should not be used in a modern system of law".[96]

86. The Law Commission's proposals and the Home Office's 2000 consultation paper used the term "corporate *killing*" rather than "corporate *manslaughter*". The former expression stemmed from the Law Commission's proposals to replace the law on involuntary manslaughter in general with crimes of "reckless killing" and "killing by gross carelessness" (see para 17).

87. JUSTICE pointed out that following the Law Commission and Home Office's forthcoming review of the law of murder, the scope of the common law of "involuntary manslaughter" might change and the word "manslaughter" might no longer even be used.[97] However, on balance, they believed that the introduction of a Corporate Manslaughter Bill should not wait for the review of the law of murder, as reform was not certain and, if undertaken, was likely to be a very lengthy process.[98]

88. **We are satisfied that the title of the offence should be "Corporate Manslaughter" not "Corporate Killing".**

---

96 Volume II, Ev 55-56

97 Volume II, Ev 310-311

98 Volume II, Ev 311

4 Causation

89. When the Law Commission published its draft Bill on Involuntary Homicide in 1996 it included a specific clause dealing with causation. This stated that a management failure by a corporation "may be regarded as a cause of a person's death notwithstanding that the immediate cause is the act or omission of an individual."[99] The Law Commission believed that such express provision was necessary in order to make it clear that the ordinary principles of causation for homicide were applicable to the corporate offence. Accordingly, a jury could find that a corporation's management failure was the cause of death despite an intervention by an individual, for example the deliberate failure of an unsupervised front-line operator. The Law Commission argued that "there is a danger that, without [this provision]... the application of the ordinary rules of causation would in many cases result in a management failure being treated as a "stage already set", and hence not linked in law to the death".[100]

90. The present draft Bill does not include the Law Commission's original clause, although the Home Office stated that the "ordinary rules of causation will apply" in determining whether a management failure has caused a victim's death.[101] The stated grounds for this decision are that case law has developed since the Law Commission reported in 1996 and a separate provision on causation is no longer needed.[102] The Government believes that the current position on causation means that an "intervening act will only break the chain of causation if it is extraordinary – and we do not consider that corporate liability should arise where an individual has intervened in the chain of events in an extraordinary fashion causing the death, or the death was otherwise immediately caused by an extraordinary and unforeseeable event".[103]

91. Although some witnesses supported the Government's position on causation,[104] a significant number urged that the Law Commission's original clause should be resurrected in the draft Bill. Disaster Action warned that without the clause it "may be extremely difficult for the prosecution to persuade a jury to convict a corporation of manslaughter".[105] The British Vehicle Rental and Leasing Association were unsure whether the draft Bill changed the current common law position on causation.[106]

92. The Law Reform Committee of the Bar Council submitted that although the Government had asserted that case law had changed since the Law Commission's report, the inclusion of a causation clause "would give statutory effect to the development in the case law and have the merit of clarity within the provisions specifically drafted for the

99 Law Commission, *Legislating the Criminal code: Involuntary Manslaughter: Item 11 of the Sixth Programme of Law Reform: Criminal Law: Report No 237*, HC (1995-96) 171, clause 4(2)(b)

100 Law Commission, HC (1995-96) 171, para 8.39

101 Home Office, *Corporate Manslaughter: The Government's Draft Bill for Reform*, Cm 6497, March 2005, para 49

102 *Draft Corporate Manslaughter Bill*, para 50

103 *Draft Corporate Manslaughter Bill*, para 51

104 Volume II, Ev 47 and 84

105 Volume II, Ev 70

106 Volume II, Ev 14

purpose of corporate manslaughter".[107] Furthermore, the Bar Council suggested that including the clause would support the Government's aim that the management failure test:

"focuses on the way in which a particular activity was being managed or organised. This means that organisations are not liable on the basis of any immediate, operational negligence causing death, or indeed for the unpredictable, maverick acts of its employees. Instead, it focuses responsibility on the working practices of the organisation"[108]

93. Since publication of the draft Bill the Law Commission has stated that although the clause does add "some value" they "do not regard this point as one of major importance".[109]

94. Although we agree with the Government that the courts have stated that only abnormal and extraordinary events will break the causal chain,[110] we are not convinced that this principle will be of general application or applied to cases of corporate manslaughter. Even if the Home Office is correct in its assertion that case law has developed and clarified the law of causation, we believe there is merit in stating the position for the corporate offence on the face of the legislation. We agree with the argument put forward by, amongst others, the Bar Council, that, if the common law were to change, it could change in a direction making it difficult to secure a conviction for the offence of corporate manslaughter.[111] **We recommend that the Government provide certainty on the law of causation, as it applies to corporate manslaughter, by including the Law Commission's original clause in the Bill.**

---

107 Volume II, Ev 118

108 Volume II, Ev 118

109 Volume II, Ev 262

110 Environmental Agency (formerly National Rivers Authority) v Empress Car Co (Abertillery) Ltd [1999] 2 AC 22.

111 Volume III, Q 81 [Mr Donnellan]

5 Relevant duty of care

Law of negligence

95. The draft Bill proposes that the offence should be based on the gross breach of a duty of care owed by the organisation to the deceased. The concept of a "duty of care" has been developed by the civil courts in the context of the law of negligence. The question of whether a "duty of care" does exist is generally determined by reference to three broad criteria: (a) is the damage foreseeable? (b) is the relationship between the defendant and victim sufficiently proximate? (c) is it fair just and reasonable to impose such a duty?

96. The civil law concept of a "duty of care" is expressly adopted in the draft Bill which states that a "relevant duty of care" … means a duty owed under the law of negligence".[112] The Home Office justifies the use of this concept by arguing that duties owed under the law of negligence are the basis of the current common law manslaughter offence:

> "We think this provides a sensible approach because organisations will be clear that the new offence does not apply in wider circumstances than the current offence of gross negligence manslaughter, to which all companies and other corporate bodies are already subject."[113]

97. In oral evidence, a legal adviser at the Home Office added:

> "We were very keen to have an offence which did not impose any new standards. We do not want to rewrite the circumstances when companies ought to be taking action to safeguard people's safety, and the duty of care is a mechanism which defines that relationship and the company knows that if it could be sued for something in negligence it can be prosecuted under this offence".[114]

98. Some witnesses welcomed this approach.[115] For example. Eversheds solicitors argued that it would provide "a greater degree of consistency".[116] However, others questioned whether it was appropriate to use a civil law concept as the basis for a criminal offence.[117] The Law Society argued:

> "(it) is problematic because it is based on a dividing line between those bodies that can be sued in negligence in domestic law and those that are exempt on public policy

---

112 Clause 4

113 Home Office, *Corporate Manslaughter: The Government's Draft Bill for Reform*, Cm 6497, March 2005, para 16

114 Volume III, Q 581 [Mr Fussell]

115 Volume II, Ev 230 and 339

116 Volume II, Ev 188

117 Volume II, Ev 57 and 246, and Volume III, Ev 117 and Q 59 [Mr Bergman]. We were a little confused by the Law Commission's memorandum. The Law Commission's original proposals did not restrict the offence to duties of care owed under the law of negligence. The Commission then argued that "the terminology of "negligence" and "duty of care" is best avoided within the criminal law because of the uncertainty and confusion that surround it" However, the Law Commission's memorandum stated: "The Government's Bill makes explicit the need for a breach of a duty of care owed to the deceased, clause 1(1). We believe this was implicit in the Commission's Bill, but we see the value of making it explicit." Ev 261

grounds. We believe that this dividing line has little meaning or justification in domestic law terms in relation to a criminal penalty".[118]

99. Moreover, some of those who submitted evidence to us were concerned by the fact that there could be cases where a death would occur as a result of a failure by senior managers which fell far below what could reasonably be expected in the circumstances and yet those circumstances would not result in a civil law "duty of care". The Centre for Corporate Accountability pointed out that this might apply in particular to cases of deaths caused by public bodies:

> "When civil law courts rule on whether or not a 'duty of care' relationship is created between a public body and a person who is suing for compensation, they quite understandably have taken into account public policy factors that relate to the fact that it is a claim for compensation. The courts have therefore given consideration to, for example, whether it is appropriate, in time and expense, for a public body to have to defend hundreds or thousands of compensation claims and then have to pay out damages. As a result of these reasons – which are distinctive to civil liability issues - the courts have stated that certain public body activities do not raise 'duty of care' relationships".[119]

100. The Centre for Corporate Accountability gave an example of a Court of Appeal ruling in the case of *Wacker*[120] - the prosecution of a driver for the manslaughter of 58 immigrants who suffocated to death in the back of his lorry while being illegally smuggled into the country. In the original case, the driver's defence lawyer had argued that the driver did not owe a duty of care to the immigrants because they were part of a joint criminal act and in these circumstances under the civil law there is no duty of care (a doctrine called *ex turpi causa non oritur actio* (no lawsuit can arise from an illegal cause)). However, the Court of Appeal rejected this defence, arguing that the civil law and criminal law had different objectives and so concepts such as duty of care needed to be adapted to the different areas of law in which they were being applied. Under the Bill such an approach cannot be adopted because it is clear that whether a duty of care exists is a matter for the civil law of negligence.

101. Other witnesses argued more simply that whether a duty of care exists under the law of negligence is a highly complicated legal issue and that this was adding an unnecessary complexity to the Bill. Mr Antoniw from Thompsons Solicitors argued "the danger of bringing in the duty of care is that it provides ample opportunity for all the legalistic pedantry that might subsequently arise in court cases".[121]

102. It was suggested to us that the offence should instead be based on breaches of duties owed by statute, such as the Health and Safety at Work etc. Act 1974 and the Merchant Shipping Act 1995; or that it should be based on statutory duties *in addition* to relevant duties of care owed by an organisation under the law of negligence.[122] Statutory health and

---

118 Volume II, Ev 221

119 Volume III, Ev 117

120 [2003] 1 Cr App R 329

121 Volume III, Q 96

122 Volume II, Ev 206 and 287, and Volume III, Q 94 [Mr Antoniw] and Q 159 [Mr Waterman]

safety duties would not bring in difficult considerations of civil law concepts, as they are designed for the context of regulating corporate conduct rather than creating liability for civil law. For example, section 3(1) of the 1974 Act imposes the following duty on employers:

> "It shall be the duty of every employer to conduct his undertaking in such a way as to ensure, so far as is reasonably practicable, that persons not in his employment who may be affected thereby are not thereby exposed to risks to their health and safety".

103. Witnesses argued that these statutory duties were very clear and well established.[123] They pointed out that the current proposals failed to clarify the relationship between the duty of care and these existing statutory duties.[124] The Centre for Corporate Accountability suggested that this approach was far more rational as companies are not usually prosecuted for breaches of duty of care:

> "It would seem to me much more logical and appropriate then to ground manslaughter in relationship to those existing duties for which companies get prosecuted. Companies do not get prosecuted for breaches of duties of care, generally, so in our view it makes much more sense for the new offence to be grounded on statutory legislation which is broader and is also much better understood than civil law duties of care".[125]

104. We accept that the definition of the offence needs to make clear which are the circumstances in which an organisation has an obligation to act, and in which a serious breach of that obligation leading to death could make it liable for prosecution for corporate manslaughter. We are not, however, convinced that this clarity would be achieved by the proposal to limit the scope of the offence to those situations in which an organisation owes a duty of care in negligence. This legal concept is unclear and is not fixed – the situations in which a duty of care may be owed in negligence will develop in accordance with judicial decisions. Furthermore, we consider that different rules should apply to determine when a person owes a duty of care for another's health and safety in the context of liability for damages under the civil law and in the context of liability under the criminal law.

105. **We propose that the Home Office should remove the concept of 'duty of care in negligence' from the draft Bill and return to the Law Commission's original proposal that the offence should not be limited by reference to any existing legal duties but that an organisation should be liable for the offence whenever a management failure of the organisation kills an employee or any other person affected by the organisation's activities. We also recommend that whether an organisation has failed to comply with any relevant health and safety legislation should be an important factor for the jury in assessing whether there has been a gross management failure. Organisations are already required to comply with duties imposed under such legislation and so should already be familiar with them.**

---

123 Volume III, Q 163[Mr Welham] and Volume II, Ev 9

124 Volume II, Ev 9

125 Volume III, Q 60 [Mr Bergman]

Categories of relationship

106. Under the common law, the situations in which a duty of care could be considered to exist are not fixed. The draft Bill, however, adds a further requirement not in the civil law of negligence, that in order to establish that a duty of care is owed it must fall under the following categories:

"(a) to its employees as such,

(b) in its capacity as occupier of land, or

(c) in connection with –

(i) the supply by the organisation of goods or services (whether for consideration or not), or

(ii) the carrying on by the organisation of any other activity on a commercial basis".[126]

While the common law includes these categories, other categories could be developed. The Home Office gave no justification in the introduction to the draft Bill for these categories being included.

107. While some witnesses stated that they were not concerned about the inclusion of these categories, others argued that they were limiting[127] and might lead to some negligent deaths being exempt.[128] We heard particular evidence that the Home Office's use of the word "supply" in 4(c)(i) would exempt certain services *provided* but not *supplied* by the State. David Bergman, Director of the Centre for Corporate Accountability told the Sub-committees that the Home Office had explained to him that the use of this word would exclude services that are provided by "the Police or the Prison Service or law enforcement bodies, inspection agencies".[129] This was confirmed to us in oral evidence by a Home Office official who told us:

"The list of relevant factors is…intended to draw a bright line so as to exclude some potential public sector duties where there is more uncertainty as to when duties of care are owed".[130]

108. **If the Government does decide to continue to base the offence on duties of care owed in negligence we do not believe the common law concept concerned should be limited by introducing categories where a duty of care must be owed. We are particularly concerned that the material accompanying the draft Bill did not highlight the use of the word "supply" and its intended purpose of automatically excluding certain activities "provided" by the state.**

---

126 Clause 4(1)

127 Volume II, Ev 141

128 Volume II, Ev 246

129 Volume III, Q 61

130 Volume III, Q 584 [Mr Fussell}

109. We discuss the exemption that arises as a result of the use of the word 'supply' further in chapter 10.

Corporate groups

110. The question of how the offence would apply in the context of groups of companies was raised in a number of submissions. In its 2000 consultation paper, the Government invited comments on whether it should be possible to take action against parent or other group companies if it could be shown that their own management failures were a cause of a death. The Government reported that "a large majority of witnesses agreed with this proposal, but in most cases on the basis that the parent company should only be liable where their own management failings had been a direct cause of death".[131] It explained the position taken in the draft Bill as follows:

"a parent company (as well as any subsidiary) would be liable to prosecution where it owed a duty of care to the victim in respect of one of the activities covered by the offence and a gross management failure by its senior managers caused death".[132]

111. We heard mixed evidence on this proposal. Some witnesses expressed concerns, including:

- that it was inconsistent with the principle of limited liability;[133]

- that it could threaten inward investment;[134]

- that it should not be possible for two companies within the same group to be prosecuted for the same deaths as this could result in shareholders being punished twice;[135] and

- that this proposal might discourage large groups from organising, managing and implementing health and safety on a group-wide basis.[136]

112. However, others supported the Government's position.[137] The Royal Academy of Engineering, for example, submitted that:

"The proposal to make a parent company liable to prosecution is, on the whole, acceptable. If the parent company ignores the behaviour of a subsidiary, or even pressurises it to cut corners, the parent company is as much the cause…".[138]

113. **We agree that it should be possible to prosecute parent companies when a gross management failure in that company has caused death in one of their subsidiaries.**

131 *Draft Corporate Manslaughter Bill*, para 37

132 *Draft Corporate Manslaughter Bill*, para 37

133 Volume II, Ev 41, 91, 240 and 273

134 Volume II, Ev 91 and 214

135 Volume II, Ev 190, 212, 224 and 240

136 Volume II, Ev 240, 273, 275 and 328

137 Volume II, Ev 212 and 224 and Volume III, Q 193 [Mr Nelson]

138 Volume II, Ev 224

114. We are therefore concerned by evidence we received which claims that it may not actually be possible to prosecute a parent company under the draft bill as the law on the duty of care in negligence currently stands. Serco-Ned Railways, for example, pointed out that "there is no established principle in English law that a parent company does in fact owe the relevant duty of care necessary as a component to the offence".[139] The Centre for Corporate Accountability also made this point and argued that the Home Office's statement that parent companies could be liable to prosecution is therefore "a rather misleading and disingenuous assertion".[140] Further, they pointed out, the only legal obligation that parent companies have is that imposed by section 3 of the Health and Safety at Work Act.

115. **We are concerned by the suggestion that it may not be possible to prosecute parent companies under the current law, as courts have not ruled that parent companies have a duty of care in relation to the activities of their subsidiaries. This is an additional argument in favour of our recommendation that the offence should not be based on civil law duties of care.**

Contractual relationships

116. A number of organisations questioned whether contractors would owe a duty of care in relation to the activities of their sub-contractors or whether employment agencies would owe a duty of care in relation to agency workers killed in the workplace.[141] The Confederation of British Industry believed that the "different legal and practical structures of corporations will give rise to different answers to… the organisation that owes the duty of care to the victim" and warned that this "inevitable inconsistency risks discrediting the law".[142]

117. The British Maritime Association also expressed concern that the law would not cover companies which provide professional management services to a company for a fee. This, they pointed out, was a common arrangement in the shipping industry.[143]

118. Ms Anne Jones, whose son died on his first day of work after signing on at an employment agency, told the Sub-committees:

> "Everyone knows that on a big construction site, like Wembley, for instance, there are enormous numbers of contractors and sub-contractors that are taking on agency workers and even agencies that have borrowed workers from other agencies. There was one case, I think it was two years ago, of an Eastern European who had been killed on a construction site and there were enormous problems with identifying who was employing him, because each layer was passing the buck, saying, "He's not

139 Volume II, Ev 328

140 Volume III, Ev 118

141 Volume III, Q 384 [Mr Roberts] and Volume II, Ev 234

142 Volume II, Ev 252

143 Volume II, Ev 327

our employee."… Unless we can tighten that up, in the first place, this bill has got a real problem on its hands".[144]

119. **We believe that, where a death of an agency worker or of an individual in a sub-contracting company was caused by a gross management failure by an employment agency or main contractor, it should be possible to prosecute these organisations jointly to establish either collective or individual corporate liability. We urge the Government to ensure that the Bill provides for this.**

120. The Union of Construction Allied Trades and Technicians argued that on a construction site the *only* company that should be liable to prosecution is the main contractor:

> "decisions about the overall standards on the site lie with the principal contractor and it is they who should be held responsible whether or not they actually employ any staff".[145]

In a similar vein, Ms Anne Jones argued that employment agencies should have primary responsibility for employment agency workers:

> "If only we could insist on saying to an agency, which effectively is a sub-contractor supplying labour, "Right, you are the principal employer, health and safety law says that you are responsible,"…until we tighten up this, placing a responsibility plainly on the people sending out the workers, then all that will happen is that the host employer will argue, "This isn't my duty of care, this isn't my responsibility," and they will walk free".[146]

121. Under the Construction (Design and Management Regulations) 2003, principal contractors are obliged to co-ordinate and manage health and safety during the construction work, developing a health and safety plan before work starts on site and then keeping it up to date throughout the construction phase. Employment agencies are responsible for an employee's training and health and safety at work, but it is the responsibility of the host employer to provide a safe system of work.

122. **We believe that principal contractors and employment agencies should take responsibility for the health and safety conditions of their sub-contractors and workers but that it is a step too far to provide that they should always be liable when a death has occurred.** Mr Commins from the Construction Confederation told the Sub-committees: "If a main contractor had carried our all the good practices and the subcontractor had just blatantly disregarded them, I do not see how you could hold the main contractor totally responsible for the subcontractor's actions".[147] We agree. **Principal contactors and employment agencies should only be liable when their own management failure is at fault. Anything more than this might encourage sub-contracting companies and those employing agency workers to ignore their health and safety responsibilities.**

---

144 Volume III, Q 14

145 Volume II, Ev 8

146 Volume III, Q 14

147 Volume III, Q 226

6 Management failure

123. At the core of the proposed new offence of corporate manslaughter is a failure "in the way in which any of the organisation's activities are managed or organised by its senior managers".[148] We discuss the restriction of this failure to that by senior managers in the following chapter (Chapter 7). This chapter considers the concept of "management failure" expressed in the phrase "the way in which any of the organisation's activities are managed or organised". This phrase first appeared in the Law Commission's proposals (see para 18). The Home Office describes it as:

> "an approach that focuses on the arrangements and practices for carrying out the organisation's work, rather than any immediate negligent act by an employee (or potentially someone else) causing death".[149]

124. As noted in para 13 above, the proposal to move away from the identification principle, the basis of liability under the common law offence, was welcomed by most witnesses. Some, however, raised concerns about the concept of "management failure" which has replaced it. The Association of Personal Injury Lawyers, for example, believed that the draft Bill failed to clarify that "management failure" includes omissions as well as actions:

> "APIL is concerned that the definition of the offence contained within section 1(1) fails to appreciate instances where "senior managers" do not "manage" or "organise" activities, which eventually leads to a death. For example, a "senior manager" who does not in any way manage or organise the appropriate health and safety precautions for his employees may be exempt in respect of the offence as currently drafted because misfeasance is covered but nonfeasance is not".[150]

125. Some witnesses did not believe that "management failure" should be the basis of the offence. They preferred different approaches based on models for attributing liability in Canadian and Australian law (see table below).[151]

> In Canadian law the conduct of the company's **"representatives"** (which includes employees, members, agents or contractors, as well as directors and partners), rather than its management, is the first consideration when determining liability. The offence is committed if, at the same time, senior officers who have responsibility for the aspect of the organisation's activities relevant to the offence have departed from a standard of care that could have been reasonably expected in the circumstances.[152]

---

148 Home Office, *Corporate Manslaughter: The Government's Draft Bill for Reform*, Cm 6497, March 2005, clause 1(1)

149 *Draft Corporate Manslaughter Bill*, para 14

150 Volume II, Ev 244

151 Volume II, Ev 10 and 69

152 The relevant section of the Canadian Criminal Code reads: "In respect of an offence that requires the prosecution to prove negligence, an organization is a party to the offence if

(a) acting within the scope of their authority

(i) one of its representatives is a party to the offence, or

(ii) two or more of its representatives engage in conduct, whether by act or omission, such that, if it had been the conduct of only one representative, that representative would have been a party to the offence; and

> Under the Australian federal Criminal Code Act 1995 (Commonwealth) liability can be attributed to a corporation where it is established either that a "corporate culture existed within the body corporate that directed, encouraged, tolerated or led to non-compliance with the relevant provision", or where the corporation failed to create and maintain a corporate culture that ensured legal compliance. Corporate culture is defined in the Act as "an attitude, policy, rule, course of conduct or practice existing within the body corporate generally or in the part of the body corporate in which the relevant activities takes place." Liability can be imputed where an individual committed the unlawful act reasonably believing that an authoritative member of the corporation would have authorized or permitted the commission of the offence.[153]

126. Disaster Action, for example, preferred the concept of "corporate culture" used in the Australian Criminal Code. They wrote:

> "In the case of The Herald of Free Enterprise, it may have been difficult for the prosecution to prove, beyond any reasonable doubt, that the way in which the organisation's activities were actively organised by its senior managers caused the deaths, rather than the act of the individual boson. It would have been possible to establish, however, the existence of a corporate culture that tolerated or led to non-compliance with health and safety provision".[154]

127. We have taken the pragmatic approach that since management failure has been the basis of proposals for a statutory offence of corporate manslaughter in the UK since 1996, it is probably too late to start to consider an entirely new model, such as one based on corporate culture, for such legislation. We note that this practical view has also been taken by the Centre for Corporate Accountability, who told us in oral evidence:

> "What you have got to recognise is the way this debate has developed in Britain. In 1994 the Law Commission came out with its First Report and then in 1996 was the key Law Commission Report which proposed a new offence of corporate killing and the concept of management failure was inherent in that particular Law Commission Bill. The Government in 2000 then supported that Law Commission Bill. Our view is that there are alternative ways of creating a new offence. In Australia the concept of "corporate culture" is used, in America a vicarious liability with a due diligence test is used. These are all perfectly possible tests that could apply but we are a practical organisation and clearly we had to engage with what was the offence that was really being discussed at the heart of Government and that was the offence which had the concept of management failure. Therefore, we have been looking at that offence, looking at management failure".[155]

128. We also believe that merely adopting models from other jurisdictions, with entirely different legal regimes, would be fraught with difficulties. We note that only one

---

(b) the senior officer who is responsible for the aspect of the organization's activities that is relevant to the offence departs - or the senior officers, collectively, depart - markedly from the standard of care that, in the circumstances, could reasonably be expected to prevent a representative of the organization from being a party to the offence."

Canadian Criminal Code Act, Section 22.1

153 Australian Criminal Code Act 1995, Section 12

154 Volume II, Ev 69

155 Volume III, Q 55 [Mr Bergman]

jurisdiction in Australia, its smallest jurisdiction, the Australian Capital Territory, has actually incorporated identical provisions to the Australian Code.

129. However, while we do not believe that the concept of management failure should be abandoned, we believe that one option the Government should consider when deciding how to overcome the problems of the senior manager test (see Chapter 7 below) is whether the draft Bill might benefit from introducing the concept of "corporate culture" *in addition* to that of management failure as a factor that juries should be permitted to consider when determining whether there has been a gross management failure. We believe it should. This is discussed further in Chapter 9.

7 Senior managers

130. The draft Bill only focuses on the way in which the organisation's activities have been managed or organised by its senior managers – management failures lower down in the organisation are not relevant. This "senior manager test" marks a departure from the Law Commission's proposals which looked more generally at failures in the way a company's activities were managed or organised, regardless of the level of management responsible for the failure (see para 18).

131. The Home Office has justified its decision to focus only on senior management failures on the grounds that the offence is designed to criminalize "truly corporate failings in the management of risk, rather than purely local ones".[156] In other words, the Home Office is aiming to target management failings that they believe can be fairly associated with the organisation as a whole. Management failures which are not the responsibility of an organisation's "senior managers" are not considered to be at a high enough level within the organisation to render the organisation itself liable for corporate manslaughter.

132. The senior manager test was the most widely criticised aspect of the draft Bill. We discuss the concerns raised below.

Delegation of health and safety loophole

133. Many witnesses, including an eminent judge, expressed concern that by restricting the offence to a level of "senior managers", the proposals would encourage large companies to delegate health and safety responsibilities to non-senior manager levels in order to avoid corporate liability.[157] The Centre for Corporate Accountability commented, "Of course, if you were a good corporate lawyer, that is what you would be suggesting".[158]

134. It was put to us in evidence that such delegation of health and safety would be seen as senior management failure in itself.[159] However, JUSTICE and the Centre for Corporate Accountability pointed out that if the decision to delegate or the supervision of the delegation was in itself not grossly negligent then the company could not be prosecuted, however serious the management failure was within the company.[160] Ms Sally Ireland, from JUSTICE, told us:

> "It would be hard to establish gross negligence on that basis unless the person to whom you were delegating was evidently incompetent to carry out the functions you were delegating to them. Remember, we are talking about the criminal standard of proof here as well. It would always be open to the senior manager to say, "He was

---

156 Home Office, *Corporate Manslaughter: The Government's Draft Bill for Reform*, Cm 6497, March 2005, para 14

157 Volume II, Ev 7, 13, 16, 19, 56, 60-61, 81, 86, 111, 132, 187, 198, 200, 211 and 220 and Volume III, Q 501 [Lord Justice Judge]

158 Volume III, Q 56 [Mr Bergman]

159 Volume III, Q 89 [Mr Donnellan], Q 268 [Mr Day] and Q 376 [Mr Roberts]

160 Volume II, Ev 167 and Volume III, Q 57 [Mr Bergman] and Q 480 [Ms Ireland]

qualified to do the job. He was perfectly responsible and we took the decision that health and safety should be determined at factory level" which sounds reasonable".[161]

135. The Centre for Corporate Accountability also highlighted a survey commissioned by the Health and Safety Executive to find out whether companies had appointed a director in charge of health and safety. It had found that:

> "In relationship to those companies that had delegated responsibility down, one of the main reasons why the companies had done that was because of the forthcoming corporate manslaughter legislation".[162]

136. **We are very concerned that the senior manager test would have the perverse effect of encouraging organisations to reduce the priority given to health and safety.**

Reintroducing the identification principle

137. Another concern raised in evidence was that the senior manager test was reintroducing the problems of the identification principle, with the requirement of identifying a directing mind simply being replaced by that of identifying senior managers.[163] Ms Sally Ireland from JUSTICE argued:

> "There is too much reference to individuals here…The offence as currently drafted is a sort of hybrid. It punishes the organisation but refers you again and again to individuals and their activities".[164]

138. The Home Office's introduction to the draft Bill claimed that its proposals are more sophisticated. It argued:

> "This does not mean that we have replaced the requirement to identify a single directing mind with a need to identify several, nor does it involve aggregating individuals' conduct to identify a gross management failure. It involves a different basis of liability that focuses on the way the activities of an organisation were in practice organised or managed".[165]

139. However, many witnesses could not see how liability would be imposed under this offence, except on the basis of aggregating the conduct of senior managers. The British Vehicle and Rental Licensing Association wrote:

> "it remains unclear to us how in practice the courts will interpret this…Further clarity is required on how…liability will be imposed other than on the basis of some form of aggregation".[166]

---

161 Volume III, Q 480

162 Volume III, Q 56 [Mr Bergman]

163 See, for example, Volume II, Ev 13, 198, 211 243-244, 269, 284, and 311.

164 Volume III, Q 478

165 Home Office, *Corporate Manslaughter: The Government's Draft Bill for Reform*, Cm 6497, March 2005, para 27

166 Volume II, Ev 13

140. We agree that the offence does appear simply to broaden the identification doctrine into some form of aggregation of the conduct of senior managers. This is a fundamental weakness in the draft Bill as it currently stands. By focusing on failures by individuals within a company in this way, the draft Bill would do little to address the problems that have plagued the current common law offence.

"Senior manager" definition

141. Many witnesses believed the restriction of the offence to senior managers would cause legal argument about who did and did not fall under the definition of "senior manager". It was feared that this legal argument might even replace the difficulties of identifying a "directing mind" under the current common law.[167]

142. The draft Bill proposes the following definition of senior manager:

"A person is a "senior manager" of an organisation if he plays a significant role in:

(a) the making of decisions about how the whole or a substantial part of its activities are to be managed or organised, or

(b) the actual managing or organising of the whole or a substantial part of those activities".[168]

This definition incorporates both senior strategic decision-makers and senior operational managers. It has two tests for seniority – first, the person must make decisions about or manage or organise a whole or substantial part of the organisation; and second, the person must play a significant role in decision-making or operational management.

143. Some of the evidence submitted to us suggested that the definition was appropriate, arguing, for example, that a clearer definition was impossible, given the large number of different organisational structures in businesses, and would have to be developed and refined by case law;[169] or that it was desirable to avoid narrowing the definition.[170]

144. However, most witnesses found the definition too vague.[171] The following specific aspects were particularly criticised.

145. No definition of the terms "significant" and "substantial" is given in the draft Bill itself. A large number of witnesses argued that they required further definition.[172] The then Lord Chief Justice and others questioned whether "substantial" was intended to have the narrower meaning, enshrined in criminal law, of "more than trivial" or the broader natural meaning.[173] Some witnesses wondered whether the terms would be applied by reference to

167 Volume II, Ev 4, 22, 33, 38, 52, 60, 81, 86, 111, 151, 217, 243, and 287

168 Clause 2

169 Volume II, Ev 87

170 Volume II, Ev 119

171 Volume II, Ev 10, 16, 39, 43, 54, 198, 111, 113, 200, 204, 210, 266, 273, 274, 281 and 300

172 Volume II, Ev 57, 66, 86, 108, 151, 211 and 238.

173 Volume II, Ev 57, 63 and 108

the number of staff employed, the turnover or profit or output generated, the space occupied, the importance in terms of the company's reputation or by other reasons.[174]

146. Others believed that the definition would not fit all organisational structures.[175] For example, witnesses pointed out that many businesses, especially smaller ones, tended to have informal hierarchies with blurred management, possibly based on family relationships or friendship,[176] and that in such organisations the position could change even during the course of a single day.[177]

147. Some of the evidence submitted to us expressed concern that individuals who ought to count as "senior managers" would not fall under the definition.[178] Examples given included: (a) clinical managers who were responsible for one area of delivery but would not play a significant role in the making of decisions or operating the whole or substantial part of the NHS; and (b) managers of large construction sites or factories belonging to a company which controlled many such sites[179] (see 'Inequitable application' paras 150 to 154).

148. On the other hand, other witnesses felt that the definition had too broad an application,[180] arguing for example that the definition should only apply to those who manage activities rather than make decisions, as this test was well established in other areas of law.[181] Some suggested that the definition would allow relatively junior levels of management to be treated as senior management whereas it should only apply to those who can make "strategic" decisions, and not those who "organise" activities.[182]

149. **We are greatly concerned that the senior manager test will introduce additional legal argument about who is and who is not a "senior manager".**

Inequitable application

150. A further criticism of the restriction of the offence to failures by senior managers was that it would apply inequitably to small and to large organisations. The Home Office has admitted that management responsibilities that might fall under the definition in a smaller organisation, such as a retail outlet or factory, might well be at too low a level in a much larger organisation.[183]

151. Some of the memoranda we received commented that such variation in application would replicate one of the main criticisms of the existing law: that it is currently easier to

---

174 Volume II, Ev 65 and 189

175 Volume II, Ev 60, 217 and 263

176 Volume II, Ev 41, 113 and 211

177 Volume II, Ev 130 and 210

178 Volume II, Ev 81, 111, 229, and 266

179 Volume II, Ev 22, 167-168 and 233

180 Volume II, Ev 271

181 Volume II, Ev 79

182 Volume II, Ev 238

183 *Draft Corporate Manslaughter Bill,* para 30

prosecute smaller organisations successfully, as management failure at a site controlled by a small firm could result in liability while the same failure at a site controlled by a larger firm might not.[184] Southlands Nursing Home, for example, wrote about the

> "irony …that by aiming at senior management to catch larger organisations, it actually focuses on smaller firms".[185]

152. We accept that, under the approach taken by the Home Office, some variation in the application of the offence is inevitable and in some cases can be appropriate. For example, it might not be fair to associate a failure by a manager of a very small section of a very large company with the company as a whole, but if this section were the totality of a small company then it might seem just to do so.

153. However, we believe that, in other cases, it does not seem right that a large company should escape liability when a smaller company does not. One such example was drawn to our attention by the Centre for Corporate Accountability and others.[186] This is the case where a person dies in a factory and investigation shows that there had been a very senior management failure that caused the death, which was the responsibility of the most senior people in that particular factory. If this factory were the only unit of business in a small company, the company would be liable. However, if the factory was one of ten owned by a company, it might not be prosecuted (depending on the interpretation of "substantial" – see "senior manager" definition" paras 141-149), unless gross negligence could be shown at head office level.[187] We agree with the Simon Jones Memorial Campaign that this "is setting the bar too high".[188]

154. However, we accept that all these examples are difficult and that others may come to different conclusions. **We believe that the Government should be aiming for an offence that applies equitably to small and large companies.**

Reputations

155. Some witnesses also argued that restricting the offence to failures by senior managers would be unfair as it would mean that the reputations of the responsible senior managers would effectively face trial without their having the power even to make representations in the proceedings.[189] The Confederation of British Industry, for example, wrote:

> "the inevitable position is that those individuals are to an extent going to be examined as if they themselves were on trial. However, because they are not defendants themselves (unless prosecuted for manslaughter or under the HSWA Act

184 Volume II, Ev 22, 63, 81,140, 197, 198, 220 and 311

185 Volume II, Ev 197

186 Volume II, Ev 22, 81 and 311

187 Volume II, Ev 167

188 Volume II, Ev 81

189 Volume II, Ev 131-132 and 252-253

as individuals) they will have no locus before the court to defend or put forward explanations for their actions or omissions".[190]

156. Others also raised concerns that the senior manager test might discourage unpaid volunteers, such as those on Housing Associations or governing bodies of schools, from taking on such roles.[191] The Seren Group and Alarm even warned that the draft Bill might result in a "recruitment crisis". Both added that it would be useful if guidance on volunteer boards could form part of the legislation.[192]

157. Some concerns were also raised that it would discourage candidates for election to councils from standing, as such members only receive an allowance.[193] However, South East Employers noted that the draft Bill had taken "the unique position of a local authority into account" (see "Public policy decisions of public authorities" in Chapter 10).

158. **We note that the reference to senior managers might also have the unfortunate effect of discouraging unpaid volunteers from taking on such roles.**

Alternatives to the senior manager test

159. We agree with many of the concerns raised about the proposal in the draft Bill that only failures in the way an organisation's activities are organised or managed "by its senior managers" would be relevant for the purposes of the offence. **We recommend that the Home Office reconsiders the underlying "senior manager" test.**

160. As we have already argued (see Chapter 6 above), we believe the offence should continue to be based on the concept of "management failure". Many witnesses believed this would be sufficient and argued that the Home Office should have retained the Law Commission's proposals.[194] These looked more generally at failures in the way a company's activities were managed or organised, regardless of the level of management responsible for the failure.

161. However, we also heard evidence from the Trades Union Congress and the Centre for Corporate Accountability, that these original proposals might have been too broad.[195] The Centre for Corporate Accountability pointed out that they could have meant that management failure even at supervisory level could result in prosecution of the company.[196] We agree that it does not seem fair to prosecute a company for a management failure at this level.

162. In oral evidence to the Sub-committees, the Parliamentary Under-Secretary of State at the Home Office appeared to accept that there might be difficulties with the senior manager test and expressed the hope that our process of pre-legislative scrutiny might elicit

---

190 Volume II, Ev 252

191 Volume II, Ev 29-30 and 149

192 Volume II, Ev 29 and 149

193 Volume II, Ev 37, 134, 200, 279 and 305

194 Volume II, Ev 8 and 23

195 Volume II, Ev 17 and 154

196 Volume II, Ev 154

an alternative to this test which did not reintroduce the problem with the original Law Commission's proposals:

> "I suppose one of the things that I was hoping was that your scrutiny might help us to deal with this problem, …you are quite right that the Law Commission's initial arrangement could potentially capture some supervisory level, a shop manager or someone, who is merely following the standard company procedure, and that is not what we intend to be the outcome of this. Is the way that we have framed the test a way which genuinely can capture the major management of an enterprise, those who are profoundly fundamentally responsible? We hope so, but if it does not then we would certainly wish it to. We did not think that management failure at a low level should be able to be caught but our aim is to make sure that wider corporate management failings, those who are actually responsible for the corporate business of the company, should be the right test…If we share a view that it should be at a senior level I would very much welcome advice on how to frame that as the kind of thing which pre-legislative scrutiny can help to drill down into and, I hope, end up with a better Bill as a result of it."[197]

163. We discuss possible alternatives below.

164. A number of organisations suggested different ways of amending the draft Bill to link it to what they considered to a "fairer" level of management at which failure should be before a company is liable for the offence.

165. Some representatives from industry argued that the failures should be targeted at "director" level, as this was a concept already recognised in the law.[198] However, we agree with the Centre for Corporate Accountability that it would be very limiting to say that a company could only be prosecuted if a director had been grossly negligent[199] and believe it would not help to solve any of the problems discussed above.

166. In its initial written evidence to the Sub-committees, the Centre for Corporate Accountability suggested adding an additional basis of liability for the offence so that a company could be prosecuted if (a) there was a grossly negligent management failure within the company that caused the death and (b) a senior manager knew or ought to have known that there was a management failure and did not take reasonable steps to rectify that failure.[200] However, as the Centre itself argued in later supplementary evidence, such a test would add further unnecessary legal complexity.[201] It would also not deal with the problem of inequitable application between small and large companies.

167. The CCA has since suggested a different approach, which redefines a "senior manager" as at "workplace level or above" and includes a concept of aggregation. It suggests that section 2 should be amended as follows:

197 Volume III, Q 568

198 For example Volume III, Q 377 [Mr Roberts] and Volume II, Ev 271.

199 Volume III, Ev 123

200 Volume II, Ev 167-168

201 Volume III, Ev 125-126

"A person is a senior manager of an organisation if:

"(1) either he plays a significant role **at a workplace level** within the company in –

(a) the making of decisions about how the whole or a substantial part of the **workplace's** activities are to be managed or organised, or

(b) the actual managing or organising of the whole or a substantial part of those activities.

(2) or is more senior than such a person"

and that section 1(1) should read:

"An organisation to which this section applies is guilty of the offence of corporate manslaughter if the way in which any of the organisation's activities are managed or organised by its senior managers–

(a) causes a person's death, and

(b) **when aggregated together,** amount to a gross breach of a relevant duty of care owed by the organisation to the deceased".[202]

168. It argues that the retention of the term "senior manager" – though at a workplace level – would prevent companies from being prosecuted as a result of gross failures at a very low level of management but that it would capture the intuitive factory examples given in para 153 above.

169. We agree with the Centre for Corporate Accountability: that a company "is not just the senior management" and that allowing grossly negligent failures at non-senior management levels to enable a company to be prosecuted is "the only way to ensure the offence can engage with complex management systems or systemic failures". However, we prefer a different alternative to the test the Centre suggests. **We believe that a test should be devised that captures the essence of corporate culpability. In doing this, we believe that the offence should not be based on the culpability of any individual at whatever level in the organisation but should be based on the concept of a "management failure", related to either an absence of correct process or an unacceptably low level of monitoring or application of a management process.** The implications of this proposal will be considered (paras 195-199) after a consideration of the draft Bill's proposals on gross breach.

8 Gross breach

170. We have already stated that we believe it is unnecessary to limit the new offence to situations where a duty of care exists. Nevertheless, in this section we consider the draft Bill's proposals in relation to a gross breach of such a duty. We believe there are some valuable ideas contained in these provisions which could be employed without dependence on a concept of duty of care.

171. Under the Government's proposals, not all breaches of a relevant duty of care owed by an organisation would be sufficient to give rise to a successful prosecution for corporate manslaughter. In its introduction to the draft Bill, the Home Office explained:

> "the new offence is targeted at the most serious management failings that warrant the application of a serious criminal offence…The offence is to be reserved for cases of gross negligence, where this sort of criminal sanction is appropriate. The new offence will therefore require the same sort of high threshold that the law of gross negligence manslaughter currently requires – in other words a **gross failure** that causes death."[203]

172. **We appreciate the reason for limiting the application of the offence to gross breaches, if utilising a concept of duty of care. This targets this serious criminal offence at the gravest management failures.**

"Falling far below"

173. The draft Bill provides that there would only be a gross breach "if the management failure in question "constitutes conduct falling far below what can reasonably be expected of the organisation in the circumstances".[204] The Government received comments in its 2000 consultation that the term "falling far below" was not, in itself, sufficiently clear. It has sought to address these concerns in the draft Bill. Clause 3 contains a list of factors which the jury must consider in deciding whether or not the conduct of an organisation has "fallen far below" what could reasonably have been expected. These are:

> "…whether the evidence shows that the organisation has failed to comply with any relevant health and safety legislation and guidance, and if so –
>
> (a)   how serious was that failure to comply;
>
> (b)   whether or not senior managers of the organisation –
>
> (i) knew, or ought to have known, that the organisation was failing to comply with the legislation or guidance;
>
> (ii) were aware, or ought to have been aware, of the risk of death or serious harm posed by the failure to comply;

203 *Draft Corporate Manslaughter Bill*, para 32

204 Clause 3(1)

(iii) sought to cause the organisation to profit from that failure".[205]

The criteria are not exclusive. Clause 3(4) adds that:

> "Subsection (2) does not prevent the jury from having regard to any other matters they consider relevant to the question."

174. The Law Society and the Association of Principal Fire Officers (APFO) believed that, even with the addition of relevant factors for a jury to consider, the "falling far below" test remained unclear. They preferred the Adomako test, which defines a gross breach as something so grossly negligent as to be criminal. This test has been criticised for being circular, but APFO argued that "[T]here is at least some case law on what constitutes "criminal" behaviour and in our view juries are more likely to be able to assess whether behaviour is "criminal" than whether it falls "far below" a standard which they themselves have to establish".[206] However, a majority of those who submitted evidence on this issue preferred the "falling far below" test.[207] This standard was originally suggested by the Law Commission in 1996.[208] Many pointed out that it is also well established as the test used for the offence of causing death by dangerous driving.[209]

Relevant factors

175. The general proposal to include a list of relevant factors for the jury to consider attracted more comment. In particular several witnesses to our inquiry read the criteria in clause 3 as conditions that had to be satisfied in order for an organisation to be liable for the offence.[210] As we read the Bill, these factors are not conditions precedent to a conviction but simply factors intended to assist a jury's consideration.

176. Others were concerned that the inclusion of relevant factors could lead to matters which are not included in them to be overlooked.[211] Ms Sally Ireland from JUSTICE, for example, argued:

> "It is however pushing a jury down the wrong route of inquiry. It also means that the prosecution will be shaped bearing in mind these factors. Defence addresses to the jury would be shaped around these factors. It could mean that you get acquittals where you should not".[212]

177. Another criticism was that clause 3(4) could mean that jurors would take into account subjective or unreliable factors.[213] One suggestion to counter this was that the list of

---

205 Clause 3(2)

206 Volume II, Ev 123-4

207 For example, Volume II, Ev 261

208 Law Commission, *Legislating the Criminal code: Involuntary Manslaughter: Item 11 of the Sixth Programme of Law Reform: Criminal Law: Report No 237*, HC (1995-96) 171, para 8.34

209 Road Traffic Act 1991 (c.40) Section 2(A)1(a). See for example, Volume II, Ev 169 and 239.

210 Volume II, Ev 17, 30, 41, 61, 82, 91, 124, 132 and 301

211 Volume II, Ev 14, 46 and 67

212 Volume III, Q 483

213 Volume II, Ev 3, 41 and 77

indicative factors should be exhaustive.[214] The Engineering Construction Industry Association proposed that clause 3(4) be amended to read, "having due regard to paragraph 2, the jury may also have regard to any other factors they consider relevant to the question".[215] However, we feel that this criticism of the current drafting of clause 3(4) unfairly assesses the capabilities of most juries. As we were reminded in one of our evidence sessions:

> "juries can be greatly underestimated. When 12 people have sat through a trial – and often they are, sadly, fairly lengthy trials – in my experience, they have grasped the issues, sometimes very quickly, sometimes with a bit of help, but often in the longer trials they are ahead of many of the lawyers before you get to the point you are going to make, because they can see it coming. Do not underestimate their ability to recognise something that is a gross failing when they see it."[216]

178. Many other witnesses welcomed the clarity provided by the list of factors to the test of "falling far below". For example, the then Lord Chief Justice submitted that the clause was "a welcome and imaginative piece of drafting".[217] Some even suggested that there should be a list of indicative factors that would indicate that the breach of the relevant duty of care was *not* gross.[218]

179. **We welcome the general proposal to include in the draft Bill an indicative, not exhaustive, list of factors which jurors are required to consider when determining whether an organisation's conduct is a gross breach. However, given the levels of apparent confusion, we would urge the Government to provide a clear explanation of how such a list of factors would be used in court.**

180. We discuss the drafting of these particular factors below.

Health and safety legislation and guidance

181. Some witnesses raised concerns about the reference to health and safety legislation in the list of factors for the jury to consider.[219] The Federation of Master Builders believed that it was unfair to proliferate health and safety legislation and then use non-compliance with these regulations as evidence to convict a company.[220]

182. There was significant concern about the reference to health and safety *guidance* in addition to legislation. Some argued that guidance was not designed to have legal force and should not be used to establish criminal liability.[221] Witnesses questioned whether the

---

214 Volume II, Ev 41

215 Volume II, Ev 3

216 Volume III, Q 100 [Mr Donnellan]

217 Volume II, Ev 109

218 Volume II, Ev 3

219 Volume II, Ev 14

220 Volume II, Ev 1

221 For example, Volume III, Q 168 [Professor Wright]

reference to guidance would include any document or piece of advice or whether it would only refer to Approved Codes of Practice or other more general guidance.[222]

183. However, others felt that it was appropriate to refer to guidance and that such concerns were misplaced. Mr Lawrence Waterman from the Institution of Occupational Safety and Health, for example, argued:

> "it would be very difficult to mount a prosecution based upon an obscure sub-clause of a leaflet that was around in a particular sector of industry for just a few months. I think when you are talking about gross breach, you mean that there is a whole sequence, that at various points management really should have availed themselves of knowledge of what was going on and recognised that it was falling below standards which similar employers in their sector, for example, were preventing happening because of the way that they managed their businesses. I think the use of the word "gross" would prevent the inappropriate prosecution based upon obscure guidance proliferating or otherwise".[223]

184. A number of local authorities and other groups believed that the reference to guidance would discourage local authorities from taking innovative approaches.[224] The Royal Borough of Kensington and Chelsea, for example, wrote:

> "The specific example in our case… relates to our recent improvements to Kensington High Street. In this case we undertook a radically new design approach and this involved disregarding Department for Transport design prescriptions whilst at the same time closely monitoring the consequences of deviation from DfT design, for personal injury accidents. To date the accident record has in fact shown an improvement. Furthermore the new improvements have received accolades and awards.
>
> Such a Bill if it becomes law could adversely affect such innovation. The proposed legislation only allows a defence to a charge of corporate manslaughter on the grounds that the defendant fully complied with health and safety requirements. This proposal in the Bill is also likely to encourage legal advisers and insurance managers to advise elected Members that they should not run the risk of departing from DfT or other Government design or other guidance".[225]

185. We note these concerns but believe they are based on a misunderstanding of the draft proposals. The close monitoring described would fall under the category of another relevant factor for the jury to consider, as they could do under section 3(4), and would therefore make it highly unlikely that a successful prosecution could be mounted in respect of such a case. It is important, however, for councils and other organisations to be liable when divergence from guidance arises from gross negligence and not from carefully monitored innovation.

---

222 Volume II, Ev 51, 151, 189-190, 198, 247 and 284

223 Volume III, Q 166

224 Volume II, Ev 135 and 260

225 Volume II, Ev 135

186. Some witnesses, by contrast, argued that the factor was not wide enough and that the jury should consider compliance with *any* relevant legislation, not just any relevant *health and safety* legislation.[226] The Working Time Directive[227] and the Food Safety Act[228] were cited as examples.

187. **We welcome the proposal in clause 3 of the draft Bill that the jury be required to have regard to whether the organisation has failed to comply with relevant health and safety legislation and guidance and that they be required to consider how serious was the failure to comply. This is an appropriate factor for juries to consider when determining whether there has been a gross management failure. We further recommend that after "legislation," the phrase "or any relevant legislation" be inserted in order to widen the scope of this factor.**

Reference to senior managers

188. Some witnesses felt that the reference to individual senior managers in the test for gross breach raised the same problems as in the senior manager test.[229] They also believed it raised practical problems. For example, Ms Sally Ireland from JUSTICE argued:

"The factors in clause 3(2)(b) refer back to senior managers, thereby incorporating some of the problems I mentioned. Are we going to have to look at all senior managers of the organisation? Probably not, but it could be open to argument. Are we going to have to look at what lots of people knew or ought to have known individually? The court time and cost in relation to that could be enormous".[230]

189. Others argued that the reference to what senior managers knew or ought to have known would be very difficult to establish as under the current law there is no legal obligation on directors to ensure that their organisation is complying with health and safety law (see "Directors' duties" in Chapter 13).[231]

190. Lord Justice Judge and the London Criminal Courts Solicitors' Association also felt that the proposal in clause 3(2)(b)(ii), which refers to awareness by senior managers of the risk of "death or serious harm", should be brought into line with the current law of gross negligence manslaughter under which there has to be gross negligence as to death only.[232]

191. **We recommend that juries should not be required to consider a factor which makes reference to senior managers in an organisation. However, if this factor is retained, we believe it should refer to the "risk of death" only and not the "risk of death or serious harm" as this would be inconsistent with the current law of gross negligence manslaughter.**

---

226 Volume II, Ev 46 and 169

227 Volume II, Ev 17, 30 and 76

228 Volume II, Ev 201

229 For example, Volume III, Q 482 [Ms Ireland].

230 Volume III, Q 482

231 Volume II, Ev 7, 23 and 258

232 Volume III, Q 491 and Volume II, Ev 140

Profit from failure

192. Clause 3(2)(b)(iii), which requires a jury to consider whether senior managers of the organisation sought to cause the organisation to profit from that failure, attracted particular comment during our inquiry. Many witnesses pointed out that this factor would be difficult to apply to public bodies.[233] Some called for the term "profit" to be replaced by "benefit".[234] The Parliamentary Under-Secretary of State at the Home Office, Fiona Mactaggart MP, welcomed this suggestion.[235] However, Sir Igor Judge argued that "You could use both almost interchangeably".[236] The Centre for Corporate Accountability suggested that the jury should instead be required to consider "the reason for the failure".[237]

193. Other evidence submitted to us called for this factor to be removed from the gross breach factors altogether.[238] The Simon Jones Memorial Campaign argued, "many of the cases that have reached public notice indicate that the main problem is a lack of care for the welfare of others".[239] Witnesses argued that profit from failure might only be relevant to the penalty imposed.[240] In oral evidence the Parliamentary Under-Secretary appeared to agree with this view, stating:

> "in my view this could be a matter which could perhaps more appropriately be dealt with in terms of its impact on sentencing rather than its impact on the criminal behaviour itself".[241]

194. **We are not convinced that the question of whether senior managers sought to cause the organisation to profit or benefit from the failure is relevant to determining whether there has been a gross breach. We therefore recommend that Clause 3(2)(b)(iii) be deleted. This factor should, however, be considered in sentencing.**

---

233 Volume II, Ev 10, 35, 46, 66, 82, 124, 132, 206, 255, 278 and 303

234 Volume II, Ev 19, 30, 61, 151 and 278

235 Volume III, Q 578

236 Volume III, Q 504

237 Volume II, Ev 169

238 Volume II, Ev 8, 24, 35, 46, 51, 71, 91, 111, 132, 137, 206, 220, 251 and 258

239 Volume II, Ev 82

240 Volume II, Ev 24, 35, 132, 206, 220 and 258

241 Volume III, Q 577

9 Gross management failure

195. We have stated (para 169) that we believe that the best way of capturing the essence of corporate culpability is to employ the Law Commission's proposed concept of a "management failure" which, following the Commission's proposals, should be defined as "conduct falling far below what can reasonably be expected of the corporation in the circumstances". Drawing on the analogy of gross negligence manslaughter we believe that such a failure is best described as a "gross management failure".

196. One of the criticisms of the Law Commission's management failure test was that it was potentially too vague. We agree with that criticism and, while rejecting the notion of a duty of care (para 105) which is crucial in clause 3, we welcome the proposed guidance in that clause aimed at aiding the jury in their determination of whether there has been a gross breach. If the concept of "duty of care" is removed from the Bill this guidance will be relevant to determining whether there has been a "gross management failure" rather than a gross breach of a duty. Some of the criteria employed in clause 3 could be a useful starting point in providing assistance to the jury.

197. In particular, and as discussed earlier (paras 181 to 187), we welcome the proposal in clause 3 of the Bill that the jury be required to have regard to whether the organisation has failed to comply with relevant health and safety legislation and guidance or any other relevant legislation and that they consider how serious was the failure to comply. This is an appropriate mechanism for assisting the jury to determine whether there has been a gross management failure. We believe, however, that the jury should be given further assistance in measuring the seriousness of the failure to comply and would recommend that they be required to consider whether a corporate culture existed in the organisation that directed, encouraged, tolerated or otherwise led to that management failure. We believe that such a consideration is the most appropriate way of assessing corporate culpability.

198. Such a provision might read as follows:

> "3. **Gross management failure**
>
> (1) A management failure is a "gross management failure" if the failure in question constitutes conduct falling far below what can reasonably be expected of the organisation in the circumstances.
>
> (2) In deciding that question the jury must consider whether the evidence shows that the organisation failed to comply with any health and safety legislation and related guidance and any other relevant legislation and, if so, how serious was the failure to comply.
>
> (3) In assessing the seriousness of the failure to comply, the jury may take account any of the following matters –
>
> (a) whether a corporate culture existed within the corporation that encouraged or tolerated non-compliance with that legislation or guidance; or

(b) whether the corporation failed to create and maintain a corporate culture requiring compliance with that legislation or guidance.

(4) In subsection (2) "health and safety legislation" means any enactment dealing with health and safety matters, including in particular the Health and Safety at Work etc Act 1974 (c.37), or any legislation made under such an enactment.

(5) In subsection (3) "corporate culture" means an attitude, policy, rule, course of conduct or practice existing within the corporation generally or in that part of the corporation where the relevant conduct occurs".

199. **We urge the Government to consider returning to the Law Commission's original proposal as a starting point. We acknowledge the argument that the Law Commission's "management failure" test could cover failings within a company that occur at too low a level to be fairly associated with the company as a whole. Nevertheless, we recommend that the Home Office should address this specific concern without abandoning the Law Commission's general approach. We suggest that juries be assisted in their task by being required to consider whether there has been a serious breach of health and safety legislation and guidance or other relevant legislation. In assessing this they could consider whether a corporate culture existed in the organisation that encouraged, tolerated or led to that management failure.**

10 Crown immunity

Removal of Crown immunity

200. The legal doctrine of Crown immunity holds that unless Parliament intends otherwise, onerous legislation does not apply to the Crown.[242] The Crown for this purpose is not limited to the monarch personally, but extends to all bodies and persons acting as servants or agents of the Crown, whether in its private or public capacity, including all elements of the Government, from Ministers of the Crown downwards. Government departments, civil servants, members of the armed forces and other public bodies or persons are, therefore, included within the scope of the immunity.

201. Clause 7 of the draft Bill expressly removes Crown immunity, making it explicit that the offence would apply to the Crown. This marks a change to the Government's 2000 Consultation Paper which proposed the retention of Crown immunity with a separate declaratory remedy for Crown bodies.[243] The introduction to the draft Bill states:

> "The Government recognises the need for it to be clearly accountable where management failings on its part lead to death. There will therefore be no general Crown immunity providing exemption from prosecution".[244]

It explains that "the Crown should not be exempt where it is in no different position to other employers or organisations". In 2000, the Government also committed itself to removing Crown immunity from statutory health and safety enforcement when Parliamentary time allowed.[245]

202. The proposal to remove Crown immunity has been widely welcomed.[246] Witnesses argued that life should be accorded the same degree of legal protection, and the bereaved the same degree of justice, regardless of whether a Crown or non-Crown body has caused a death[247] and that it is desirable, wherever possible, to enhance the accountability of public authorities in relation to deaths caused by gross negligence.[248] Other reasons given for welcoming the proposal to remove Crown immunity included the following:

- that a manslaughter conviction would produce benefits for the public in the form of a thorough review of procedures in the relevant authority;[249]

- that there should be a level playing field between the public and private sector;[250]

---

242 On the basis that legislation is made by the Sovereign in Parliament for the regulation of Her subjects, not Herself.

243 Home Office, *Reforming the Law on Involuntary Manslaughter: The Government's Proposals*, May 2000, para 3.2.8

244 Home Office, *Corporate Manslaughter: The Government's Draft Bill for Reform*, Cm 6497, March 2005, para 38

245 *Revitalising Health and Safety: Strategy Statement*, June 2000, Action Point 15

246 See for example Volume II, Ev 9, 18, 24, 31 and 133

247 Volume II, Ev 24 and 62

248 Volume II, Ev 312

249 Volume II, Ev 312

250 Volume II, Ev 90

- and that failure to apply the offence to the Crown would constitute a breach of human rights law.[251]

203. JUSTICE raised the concern that public confidence in a public authority and the services it provides could be severely undermined by the stigma of a manslaughter conviction.[252] However, it did not believe this was a reason not to extend the Bill to Crown bodies:

> "It is a slightly anomalous position for a public authority to subsist with a very serious criminal conviction against it. That applies all the more where it is a law enforcement or prosecution agency or a police force but to an extent, although it is a concern, we accept that it is perhaps more theoretical than practical and we would not use it as an argument to avoid extending the Bill to police forces because I think there are more important considerations in favour of its extension".[253]

204. **We welcome the proposal to remove Crown immunity for the offence of corporate manslaughter. However, we consider that the force of this historic development is substantially weakened by some of the broad exemptions included in the draft Bill.** We discuss these further in the section below.

205. **We also note that five years have passed since the Government committed itself to removing Crown immunity for health and safety offences. We urge the Government to legislate on this issue as soon as possible.**

Crown immunity "by the back door"?

206. A number of witnesses to our inquiry have argued that, in practice, Crown immunity has been retained in many respects because the draft Bill includes exemptions from the offence that will apply primarily to Crown bodies.[254] These exemptions are:

- exclusively public functions

- the public policy decisions of public authorities

- military activities

- services and goods "provided" by an organisation

207. We discuss these exemptions in detail below.

---

251 Volume II, Ev 24 and 313 (Articles 2, 13 and 14 of the European Convention on Human Rights)

252 Volume II, Ev 312

253 Volume III, Q 454 [Ms Ireland]

254 Volume II, Ev 32 and 164

Exclusively public functions

Lack of clarity

208. Clause 4 of the draft Bill expressly provides for two situations in which no relevant duty of care would exist. The first situation is the exercise of an "exclusively public function". This phrase is exhaustively defined in the Bill as

> "a function that falls within the prerogative of the Crown or is, by its nature, exercisable only with authority conferred –
>
> (a) by the exercise of that prerogative, or
>
> (b) by or under an enactment".[255]

209. We were unclear about exactly which situations would fall under this definition. This uncertainty was shared by witnesses to our inquiry.[256] For example, the London Criminal Courts Solicitors' Association were unsure whether police operational activities would fall under this exemption (although these activities would already be exempt as activities "provided", see "Services "provided" by the State" below).

210. A report by the Public Administration Select Committee suggests it is very difficult to determine what functions fall within the "prerogative of the Crown".[257] This view was shared by Professor Dawn Oliver, Professor of Constitutional Law at the Faculty of Laws, University College London, who submitted that there are different views in legal circles as to what functions would fall within this expression. On one narrow interpretation, the prerogative only covers the "special pre-eminence" of the Crown over and above that of private individuals, which would cover situations such as the making of treaties, the disposition of the armed forces, the granting of mercy and pardon, the dissolution of Parliament and, perhaps most importantly in this context, matters relating to national security like arming the police. A broad interpretation of the prerogative would, on the other hand, include all the powers of the Crown which are not expressly provided by statute, including, for example, the power to make contracts and to change civil service terms of employment.[258]

211. The scope of the functions encapsulated within the second limb of the definition of "an exclusively public function" is also unclear. This focuses on the difficult legal question of whether a function would "by its nature" only be exercisable with special legal authority. We heard evidence that while some examples would clearly require such authority, such as matters relating to the detention of prisoners, and others clearly would not, such as providing gas masks to members of the public, there was likely to be a substantial grey area between in which it is unclear whether a function does or does not, by its nature, require such authority.

---

255 Clause 4(1) and (4)

256 Volume II, Ev 141

257 Volume II, Ev 186 and Public Administration Select Committee, Fourth Report of 2003-04, *Taming the Prerogative: Strengthening Ministerial Accountability to Parliament*, HC 422

258 Volume II, Ev 186

212. Furthermore, Professor Oliver believed that an exclusively public function "exercisable only with authority conferred by or under an enactment" might in fact cover everything that statutory bodies did. She added that:

> "local authorities owe all their powers to enactments and it would seem to follow that local authorities and other statutory bodies are immune under the bill as it places all activities exercised under statutory authority in the category of 'exclusive public function'. I think this must be an error".[259]

213. **The definition of "exclusively public function" is unsatisfactory. If the Government does decide to retain this exemption, the definition would need further work to ensure that there is clarity about the situations in which it would apply.**

Should exclusively public functions be exempt from the offence?

214. The Government has submitted that areas which fall within the scope of "exclusively public functions" are more appropriately subject to wider forms of public and democratic accountability than the courts.[260] In response, the Transport and General Workers Union remarked that the exclusively public function exemption also applies to private bodies, which would not be subject to other forms of accountability.[261]

215. JUSTICE argued that:

> "To create such an exception is to state that in those circumstances, gross negligence causing death on the part of a corporation is lawful under the criminal law. We do not believe that gross negligence causing death can ever be justified, even in an emergency".[262]

216. The London Criminal Courts Solicitors' Association criticised the exemptions for being too broad and stated that despite the removal of Crown immunity, many Crown bodies would not be properly held to account for deaths arising out of their management failures.[263] Other witnesses also expressed scepticism about the effectiveness of alternative accountability mechanisms:

> "[E]ven if you get a finding of unlawful killing from an inquest, it does not necessarily follow someone is going to be charged, let alone convicted, of that offence. So I doubt whether in fact there are necessarily other ways in which these types of activities can properly be investigated".[264]

217. **We are very concerned by the exemption for exclusively public functions and are not convinced by the Government's arguments for including in the Bill a blanket exemption for deaths resulting from the exercise of public functions. We do not**

---

259 Volume II, Ev 187

260 Home Office, *Corporate Manslaughter; The Government's Draft Bill for Reform,* Cm 6497, March 2005, para 6

261 Volume II, Ev 24. See also Volume II, Ev 103.

262 Volume II, Ev 313

263 Volume II, Ev 142

264 Volume III, Q 113 [Mr Caplan]

consider that there should be a general exception under this heading since bodies exercising such public functions will still have to satisfy the high threshold of gross breach before a prosecution can take place, namely that the failure must be one that "falls far below what could be reasonably expected." We do not consider that a private or a Crown body should be immune from prosecution where it did not meet this standard and as a result, a death occurred.

Deaths in prisons and police custody

218. Given the uncertainties surrounding exactly what functions would fall under this exemption, we have decided to consider an area which the Government has expressly stated would be covered by this exemption: "functions relating to the custody of prisoners".[265]

219. The Government has argued that it is appropriate to exempt such functions because:

"The personal liability of individuals undertaking such functions will remain, as is proper, under the criminal law. However, organisational failings in these areas are more appropriately matters for wider forms of public and democratic accountability. Deaths in prisons are …already subject to rigorous independent investigations through public inquest before juries and through independent reports capable of ranging widely over management issue and punishable post inquest".[266]

220. The Association of Chief Police Officers welcomed the exemption for deaths in police custody. It argued:

"we have civil liability and I believe that the Independent Police Complaints Commission provides that level of scrutiny, independence and confidence in the service… we are not complacent about deaths in police custody. We are absolutely committed as a service to try to reduce the opportunity for these to occur…We are dealing with vulnerable people; people who come into our custody are vulnerable whether through mental illness, drink or drugs, and again I believe that the circumstances you are talking about there in terms of the coroner would fit very well with gross negligence manslaughter. That may be an individual act or an individual decision or poor practice that leads to a chain of events leading to someone's untimely death".[267]

221. However, the exemption for prisoners in prison and police custody also attracted a significant amount of criticism. Ms Sally Ireland from JUSTICE, for example, described it as possibly "the worst thing about the Bill".[268] Many organisations were concerned that prisoners are in a particularly vulnerable position and that since they are under the control

265 Home Office, *Corporate Manslaughter: The Government's Draft Bill for Reform,* Cm 6497, March 2005, para 22

266 *Ibid*

267 Volume III, Q 424-425 [Mr Stoddart]

268 Volume III, Q 464 [Ms Ireland]

of the state, it should, therefore, take particular care to protect their lives.[269] For example, Mr Geoff Dobson from the Prison Reform Trust told the Sub-committees:

> "It seems to us to be almost beyond belief that prisoners who are in a very powerless situation in an institution should be exempt".[270]

222. The Police Federation of England and Wales disagreed with the exemption for deaths in police custody, arguing that 'all aspects of policing should have the capability' of being liable for the offence.[271]

223. The Prison Reform Trust submitted that prosecutions for corporate manslaughter following a death in prison would not necessarily conflict with existing accountability mechanisms:

> "The exemption of the critical functions involving duty of care to prisoners, on the basis that they are subject to separate enquiries, appears to arise from a confusion of means and ends. If investigations suggest that "management failure" did, in all probability, bring about the death of an inmate, then it is difficult to understand why the offence should be less relevant than in any other sphere of service delivery. The various tests set out under 'Management failure by senior managers' and 'Gross breach and statutory criteria' would still apply, providing a transparent framework, with necessary safeguards".[272]

224. The Centre for Corporate Accountability pointed out that deaths in police custody can at least be investigated by the Independent Police Complaints Commission who can then prosecute individuals for manslaughter or for health and safety offences, while deaths in prisons are not subject to investigations that can result in criminal offences.[273] JUSTICE submitted that the exemption in the Bill might therefore breach human rights law:

"The UN Human Rights Committee, in relation to a death in custody, was of the view that a state party to the International Covenant on Civil and Political Rights was "under an obligation to take effective steps…to bring to justice any persons found to be responsible for his death".[274]

225. It was also pointed out to us that private companies running prisons or custody suites would also be exempt for matters relating to the custody of prisoners. JUSTICE questioned whether existing accountability mechanisms applied effectively to such companies:

> "In relation to private prisons, I think it is open to question what kind of accountability there really is at the moment. You may have read about recent events

---

269 Volume II, Ev 84

270 Volume III, Q 464

271 Volume III, Q 452 [Ms Berry]

272 Volume II, Ev 283

273 Volume III, Ev 121

274 Volume II, Ev 313 (Barbato v. Uruguay, Communication No. 84/1981, UN Doc Supp No. 40 (A/38/40) at 124 (1983))

whereby some of the Home Office team were not allowed into a secure training centre to investigate the use of restraints. They underline this".[275]

226. In 2004, the Joint Committee on Human Rights (JCHR) examined the issue of "Deaths in Custody".[276] It found that during a period from 1999 to 2003 "a total of 434 prisoners in England and Wales took their own lives, equivalent to *one every four day*".[277] The report stressed the importance of a good management in preventing such deaths:

"At the level of the day to day operation of prisons and other places of detention, the culture of a prison or secure hospital, the extent to which people are treated with dignity, the quality of relationships between prisoners and staff, are all critically important. This is an aspect of suicide prevention which in the healthcare setting has been termed "relational security." It is also reflected in the standard against which the Chief Inspector of Prisons inspects, of a "healthy prison", which meets standards of decency, safety, and respect".[278]

227. **We believe that there is no principled justification for excluding deaths in prisons or police custody from the ambit of the offence. The existence of other accountability mechanisms should not exclude the possibility of a prosecution for corporate manslaughter. Indeed public confidence in such mechanisms might suffer were it to do so. We are particularly concerned that private companies running prisons or custody suites, which are arguably less accountable at present, would be exempt. Accordingly, we recommend that, where deaths in prisons and police custody occur, they should be properly investigated and the relevant bodies held accountable before the courts where appropriate for an offence of corporate manslaughter.**

Public policy decisions of public authorities

228. Clause 4 of the draft Bill also provides an exemption for public authorities making decisions as to matters of public policy. The meaning of "public authority" is defined in the draft Bill as having the same meaning as in section 6 of the Human Rights Act 1998.[279] Private bodies also fall within the definition of public authority if their functions are functions of a public nature. "Matters of public policy" are not defined in the draft Bill although it does state that they include "in particular the allocation of public resources or the weighing of competing public interest".[280]

229. The Home Office stated that the proposal makes explicit the position under the current law of negligence "that public authorities will rarely owe a duty of care where decisions involve weighing competing public interests dictated by financial, economic,

275 Volume III, Q 468 [Ms Ireland]

276 Joint Committee on Human Rights, Third Report of Session 2004-5, *Deaths in Custody*, HL Paper 15-I, HC 137-I

277 *Deaths in Custody*, para 41

278 *Deaths in Custody*, para 370

279 Clause 4(4)

280 Clause 4(2)

social or political factors, which the courts are not in a position to reach a view on".[281] The Institute of Directors argued that the Government was justified in taking this approach:

"It is inevitable that in the course of making decisions about allocation of scarce resources that trade-offs have to be made across the activity of an organisation. It would be wholly unrealistic to expect decision-makers to disproportionately allocate resources to one area of activity, without taking account of other policy aims and objectives".[282]

230. However, a survey by Cameron McKenna Solicitors indicated that 97.2% of their witnesses took the opposite view and believed that public bodies should be accountable in the same way that the private sector would be. The firm submitted:

"there is no reason in principle why any public body should be in a different position when it comes to consideration of its duties in terms of the offence of corporate manslaughter".[283]

231. The Ergonomics Society questioned why the allocation of resources should provide an exemption for public bodies:

"Such issues of resource allocation and other matters are not unusual in the management of safety in commercial and industrial contexts, and so we cannot accept this as an argument for excluding 'matters of public policy'."[284]

232. The Centre for Corporate Accountability also argued against the public policy exemption.[285] Its supplementary memorandum to the Sub-committees raised a tragic example of a suicide committed in a mental health hospital which might fall under this exemption. It submitted:

"One of the main issues in this particular case relates to whether the failure to remove a particular ligature point in a room where she committed suicide (despite repeated requests from NHS Estates and others that ligature points should be removed) could be considered grossly negligent. The question that we are concerned about is whether this or similar set of circumstances might result, under the proposed public policy exemption, in the public body arguing successfully that this was a matter of public body decision making. What would be the situation if the public body, for example, stated that they did not proceed with removing ligature points as they had to balance the expense of doing this with other costs and therefore it was a matter of "the allocation of public resources"? What would have happened if for example the NHS estates had itself not provided the advice because it was the outcome of the 'allocation of public resources or the weighing of competing public interests' - although there was clear evidence that they knew about the serious risks

281 Home Office, *Corporate Manslaughter: The Government's Draft Bill for Reform,* Cm 6497, March 2005, para 23

282 Volume II, Ev 46

283 Volume II, Ev 103

284 Volume II, Ev 36

285 Volume II, Ev 158

of not removing ligature points and had been advised to instruct Health Authorities to remove them?"[286]

233. We believe that there should be an exemption for those making overarching public policy decisions, where there may be very difficult decisions about allocation of resources. Using the example given to us by the Centre for Corporate Accountability, it might indeed be the case that the Department of Health has to weigh the safety benefits of removing all ligature points from all NHS estates against the cost of directing money away from other possible initiatives, such as making a new cancer drug available. However, we do not believe it should be open to a mental health hospital to argue that it had ignored the direction of NHS estates because it had to make a cost benefit analysis which was a matter of public policy. At this level we believe the hospital should be considered to be implementing public policy and not deciding it. **We believe that there should be an exemption to the offence for public policy decisions. However, we believe that this should only apply at a high level of public policy decision-making.**

Military activities

234. Although the Ministry of Defence is an organisation for the purposes of the draft Bill, clause 10 explicitly states that certain activities of the armed forces fall outside the scope of the offence. The exempt activities are defined as:

> "(a) activities carried on by members of the armed forces in the course of or in preparation for, or directly in support of, any combat operations; [and] (b) the planning of any such operations".[287]

235. The "armed forces" is defined as "any naval, military or air forces of the Crown raised under the law of the United Kingdom".[288] "Combat operations" is broadly defined to include:

> "(a) operations, including peacekeeping operations and operations for dealing with terrorism or civil unrest, in which members of the armed forces come under attack or face threat of attack or armed resistance; and (b) training that is designed to simulate operations of a kind mentioned in paragraph (a)".[289]

236. The Government has justified this exemption as follows:

> "It is important that by applying criminal proceedings for this sort of offence to the Crown, we do not adversely affect matters of national security or the defence capability… It is also important that the ability of the Armed Forces to carry out, and train for, combat and other warlike operations is not undermined. The law already recognises that the public interest is best served by the Armed Forces being immune from legal action arising out of combat and other similar situations and from preparation for these, and this is recognised in the offence. We also consider it

---

286 Volume III, Ev 120

287 Clause 10

288 Clause 10(3)

289 Clause 10(3)

important that the effectiveness of training in conditions that simulate combat and similar circumstances should not be undermined and these too are not covered by the offence".[290]

237. A number of witnesses agreed that the exemption in the draft Bill for the armed forces was justified.[291] However, some felt the exemption was outdated and pointed out that it had been removed in other contexts, such as sex discrimination law[292] and some health and safety law cases.[293] Others argued that the military should be properly held to account for deaths arising from their management failures,[294] and that if it were not, the UK might be in breach of human rights law.[295]

238. Other witnesses considered that an exemption was appropriate in principle but that the draft Bill had drawn it too widely. The Bar Council submitted:

> "Preparation for any combat operation may well include elements of basic training, rather than specialised activities directly in support of combat operations….The removal of the words 'or in preparation for' in the clause would not alter the effect of [the] clause in respect of specialised preparation for the combat operations, because training for such operations is covered by clause [10(3)](b). It would, however, remove the exemption from the level of basic training and other activities peripheral to the training for combat operations. This may go some way towards allaying the public concern particularly in respect of the responsibility for the implementation of standards of safety of young recruits entering the armed forces".[296]

239. **Although we recognise the unique position of the armed forces, we consider that the exemption is drawn too widely. We are concerned that "preparation" for combat operations would encompass routine training and believe that such a wide exemption cannot be justified. We therefore recommend that the words "in preparation for" be removed from clause 10(1)(a) so that the exemption is restricted to combat operations and acts directly related to such operations.**

Services "provided" by the state

240. In Chapter 5, we discussed the Government's use of the term "supply" in the list of relevant duty of care categories in order to expressly exclude certain services "provided" by public bodies. There we recommended that any exemptions in the draft Bill should be made explicit, as with the three exemptions already discussed above. One example of a service that would fall into the category of being "provided" and not "supplied" would be police and fire service operations. (As discussed in para 213, there is uncertainty whether

---

290 Home Office, *Corporate Manslaughter: The Government's Draft Bill for Reform,* Cm 6497, March 2005, para 40

291 See for example, Volume II, Ev 79.

292 Volume II, Ev 57

293 Volume II, Ev 158

294 Volume II, Ev 314

295 Volume II, Ev 142 and 159

296 Volume II, Ev 120

these might also fall under the term "exclusively public function".) We discuss this particular exemption below.

The operational activities of the police and fire services

241. The Association of Chief Police Officers (ACPO) and the Association of Principal Fire Officers (APFO) agreed with the Government that their operational duties should be exempt, arguing that their operational environment placed them in a unique position compared to other public bodies. Both organisations pointed out that their operations entailed a high degree of risk. ACPO wrote: "Policing is often a very dangerous business".[297] APFO gave an example of a case in Greater Manchester where the fire service was called:

"The fire tender had been called to a lake where a young person was in the lake swimming with his friends and went under the water…The friends pointed out where they had last seen their young friend. The fire officer tied a rope around his waist and swam out while his colleagues, on the side of the lake, held on to the rope. The fire officer swam around and dived under the water looking for this young person but could not find him. He then asked the crew to pull him back and they pulled him back but the line had sunk just beneath the water and it snagged on a branch, unbeknown to him and the crew. The result was he drowned …This is the operational environmental in which the fire and rescue service operates".[298]

242. Both organisations expressed concern that extending the offence to their operational activities could lead to a risk averse service with possible dangerous consequences for members of the public. APFO, for example, added:

"The concern of the fire and rescue services is that there will be a risk-averse approach to these types of incidents. What you will instruct, in Manchester for example, is when you arrive at the side of the lake you do not enter that water until a boat arrives and so the crew will be formally instructed by their senior management not to do that until a boat arrives".[299]

243. However, the Centre for Corporate Accountability was critical of the arguments given for this exemption:

"We would like to point out a serious contradiction in ACPO's response. It says that it is happy to comply with health and safety law – and there must therefore be an assumption that health and safety law compliance does not cause any particular problems of risk averseness. ACPO also notes that individually and organisationally the police are willing to be held account for health and safety offences. If this is the case, then it is difficult to see what are the particular problems that the police would face in relation to the new offence. If they seek to comply with health and safety law – then they have nothing to fear from the new offence and it is difficult to see what additional risk averseness would exist. Senior police officers would simply have to

297 Volume III, Q 403 [Mr Stoddart]
298 Volume III, Q 412 [Mr Pritchard]
299 Volume III, Q 417 [Mr Pritchard]

64

ensure that their force complies with existing health and safety law – as presumably these senior officers seek to do now".[300]

244. The Police Federation of England and Wales took a different view to ACPO. It believed that all aspects of policing should be capable of being liable to the offence. In oral evidence Mrs Jan Berry, Chairman of the organisation, gave a strong argument by analogy that overall an extension to operational activities would have a positive impact if it was accompanied by appropriate education:

"it is not to do with death but I think it demonstrates the point. Stop and search is something which has attracted a fair amount of attention and I do not think there is any doubt that a lot of police officers stopped using stop and search in circumstances where it may have been more appropriate because of the fear of action being taken against them. There was some work undertaken in one part of the country where they actively trained police officers in stop and search powers. Following that piece of training the powers were used far more effectively than they ever had been previously and therefore the quality of the searches was much better. The arrests that came from them was much better. If you are a learning organisation, if you make sure that your training is right and use the operational experience to good effect later and you train people properly, risk aversion does not have to be taken into account".[301]

245. **We are concerned by the possibility that the inclusion of police and fire operational activities might lead to a culture of risk averseness. However, this could be countered by effective education. We believe that the Bill should be drafted so that emergency services' operational activities are only liable for the offence in cases of the gravest management failings.**

---

300 Volume III, Ev 120

301 Volume III, Q 461

11 Territorial application

Where harm occurs

246. Clause 16(1) of the draft Bill states that the offence will only apply if "harm resulting in death is sustained in England and Wales" or in territorial waters or on an offshore rig or British flagged ship or aircraft. The place where the initial harm occurs is therefore the only relevant factor. The Government has justified its restrictive approach to jurisdiction on the following basis:

> "there would be very considerable practical difficulties if we were to attempt to extend our jurisdiction over the operations abroad of companies registered in England and Wales. Such difficulties would mean that the offence would in practice be unenforceable".[302]

247. Some of the memoranda we received agreed with the Government's approach.[303] The Confederation of British Industry suggested that an even more restrictive approach should be adopted, arguing that in practice it will not be possible to impose sanctions against foreign registered companies or those where the senior management is based abroad.[304]

248. A greater number of witnesses, however, believed that the territorial application was too limited. The Trades Union Congress called for the provisions to be extended to British Dependencies, such as Bermuda, the Cayman Islands, Gibraltar and the Isle of Man, which are often used to register Merchant Shipping.[305] The Fire Brigades Union were concerned that they were being encouraged to provide firefighting at sea services and major incidents abroad and yet the offence would not apply to foreign-registered vessels or when they were working overseas.[306]

249. Particular concerns were raised about the fact that the offence would not apply where the harm results abroad but the grossly negligent behaviour has occurred in England or Wales.[307] The Transport and General Workers' Union argued that unless jurisdiction was extended in this way the new offence of corporate manslaughter would have no deterrent value for UK companies operating overseas. In other words, there would be no incentive for such companies to improve or maintain acceptable standards of health and safety in the activities they conduct abroad.[308] Other witnesses felt that this would have particular implications for southern hemisphere countries where regulatory standards, it has been argued, can be driven down by the need to attract foreign capital.[309]

---

302 Home Office, *Corporate Manslaughter: The Government's Draft Bill for Reform,* Cm 6497, March 2005, para 56

303 Volume II, Ev 121

304 Volume II, Ev 249-50

305 Volume II, Ev 17

306 Volume II, Ev 217

307 Volume II, Ev 9, 11, 17, 25, 30,36,59, 85,133, 170, 207, 220, 234, 255, 276 and 302

308 Volume II, Ev 25

309 Volume II, Ev 9 and 25

250. It was pointed out to us that British citizens, if they caused death abroad, could be prosecuted in the British courts.[310] For example, the Simon Jones Memorial Campaign submitted:

> "In common law manslaughter an individual can be prosecuted for a death which occurred abroad. We fail to see why employing organisations should be treated more leniently than individuals. While it might be difficult to prosecute in some circumstances we feel that if a senior management failure in England caused a death in say Northern Ireland or Germany, then the organisation should be prosecuted because the crime took place in England."[311]

The Occupational and Environmental Health Research Group noted that there were a range of legislative provisions (not least those covering financial wrongdoing and corruption) that enabled the prosecution of UK companies operating abroad.[312]

251. The Centre for Corporate Accountability submitted that:

> "The bizarre thing about this is that would be a much easier offence to investigate than the scenario of the management failure outside Britain with the death in Britain. It would be very difficult to investigate companies which were operating abroad; it is much easier to investigate them in Britain".[313]

252. Other memoranda we received recognised the practical limits to the scope of the Bill, but argued that the Home Office had dismissed the issue too readily. The Institution of Occupational Safety and Health acknowledged that it would be very difficult to adduce the evidence where a death had occurred abroad but wanted to see more effort invested in exploring how it might be done.[314] The Centre for Corporate Accountability suggested that incidents overseas "should be dealt with on a case by case basis".[315] Others proposed bilateral agreements or protocols with other jurisdictions.[316]

253. We believe that in principle it should be possible to prosecute a company for corporate manslaughter when the grossly negligent management failure has occurred in England or Wales irrespective of where a death occurred. If this was not the case, there would be no incentive for such companies to improve or maintain acceptable standards of health and safety in the activities they conduct abroad. We also note that there is a general trend of increased extra territorial application for crime. Money laundering and sex trafficking are two such examples. The Attorney General also recently spoke proudly of having secured a conviction of a non-British citizen for torture committed in Afghanistan (using international war crime law).[317]

---

310 Volume II, Ev 11, 170 and 220

311 Volume II, Ev 85

312 Volume II, Ev 9 and 25

313 Volume III, Q 66 [Mr Bergman]

314 Volume III, Q 171 [Mr Waterman]

315 Volume II, Ev 170

316 Volume III, Q 171 [Mr Waterman]

317 IBA conference, Prague, *'How far can laws reach? The problem of extraterritoriality',* 28 September 2005. This speech can be found at http://www.lslo.gov.uk/speeches.htm.

254. Although we accept that there may be some practical difficulties in investigating a corporate manslaughter offence when an individual has died in some jurisdictions outside the European Union, we consider that within the rest of the UK there will be no such difficulty and that in the rest of Europe there will be minimal practical limitations. **We recommend that the offence be extended so that deaths that take place in the rest of the UK are within the scope of the offence when the management failure occurred in England and Wales. We also urge the Government to make provision in the Bill for the offence later to be extended at least to cover cases where deaths have occurred in the rest of the European Union. Although we understand that evidential and jurisdictional factors mitigate against the offence applying to UK bodies operating elsewhere in the world, we consider that the Government should take to itself a power to require information from the relevant UK body about such a death.**

Relationship with the rest of the UK's law

255. The draft Bill when enacted would apply to England and Wales only.[318] The introduction to the draft Bill explains that "Criminal law in Northern Ireland is the responsibility of the Secretary of State for Northern Ireland and is a devolved matter in Scotland".[319] We heard evidence from representatives from industry that it was important that there was as little practical difference between the law in England and Wales and the rest of the UK. For example, Cameron McKenna Solicitors submitted:

> "It is regrettable that there is a separate process underway to review the law in Scotland. The Scottish law of culpable homicide for companies is already different to that of England and Wales. The government should endeavour to promote a consistent UK-wide reform".[320]

256. The Northern Ireland Office (NIO) took the view that "the same proposals should be consulted upon in Northern Ireland and, subject to that consultation, that the Bill to be brought forward in due course for England and Wales should be extended also to Northern Ireland".[321] Its deadline for consultations was 25 August 2005.

257. In Scotland, the Scottish Executive created an "Expert Group" with a remit to "review the law in Scotland on corporate liability for culpable homicide and to submit a report to the Minister of Justice by the summer, taking into account the proposals recently published by the Home Secretary".[322] The Group published its conclusions on 17 November 2005.[323] Its proposals for reform go much further than the draft Bill in certain respects. These include provisions that:

- there be created a secondary offence for directors or senior managers where their actions and omissions directly contributed to the death and a stand alone individual

318 Clause 16(1)

319, Home Office, *Corporate Manslaughter: The Government's Draft Bill for Reform*, Cm 6497, March 2005, para 63

320 Volume II, Ev 104

321 Northern Ireland Office, (2005) *Corporate Manslaughter: Northern Ireland*

322 Scottish Executive, (2005) "Expert Group on Corporate Homicide" 2005 (08/09)

323 Scottish Executive, *Corporate Homicide: Expert Group Report*, November 2005

offence which would apply to any person who causes a death through their work, without requiring that the employing organisation is guilty of corporate killing;

- the offence should apply to unincorporated bodies;

- the offence should apply to situations where the management failure took place in Scotland but the death took place abroad;

- the removal of Crown immunity should be more extensive than in the draft Bill; and

- the offence should be subject to wider penalties than fines and remedial orders.

258. The Group wrote:

> "the majority of members feel that alignment is secondary to getting the law right in Scotland. We all agree that alignment need not be on the basis of the current Home Office proposals, on which we have a number of reservations. Indeed the Group believes that the approach which we outline... provides a useful basis for amending the law in all UK jurisdictions, not just in Scotland".[324]

259. **Although we accept that it will be inevitable that there are some differences between the law on corporate manslaughter or culpable homicide in England and Wales and in Scotland because of the difference in the two legal regimes, the Government should be doing all it can to ensure there is as little practical variation as possible. We note that the recommendations in our report would bring the Government's draft Bill closer to the reforms proposed by the Scottish Expert Group.**

---

12 Sanctions

260. The draft Bill currently provides for organisations found guilty of the offence to be liable to a fine or remedial order.[325] These two different kinds of sanctions are discussed in turn below. We then consider possible alternatives.

Unlimited fines

261. The draft Bill proposes that organisations guilty of corporate manslaughter should be "liable on conviction on indictment to a fine".[326] No restrictions on the level of such a fine are provided, meaning that the level of fine which a court could impose is unlimited.[327] The Home Office's introduction to the draft Bill explains that "where the circumstances of the case merit, a fine can be set at a very high level".[328]

262. There were mixed views on the proposals for fines to be unlimited. A number of organisations believed that some restrictions needed to be set. Suggestions included basing penalties on the size and turnover of the organisation.[329] As to the level of the fine, it was suggested that "mitigating circumstances" such as past health and safety record should be taken into account.[330] Keoghs Solicitors suggested a suspended fine, related to improvements in health and safety, with a company becoming liable to an additional fine if it failed to improve within a set time.[331]

263. On the other hand, many witnesses, particularly unions and victims' groups, believed that even unlimited fines would constitute an inadequate sanction in many cases, especially where large companies were involved.[332] One reason expressed for this view was that current fines were often insignificant and therefore an inadequate deterrent. Alan Ritchie, the General Secretary of the Union of Construction Allied Trades and Technicians, gave the Sub-committees one such powerful example:

> "I go back to a case in Scotland. They were digging a trench and the site agent contacted the company and said, 'Look, this needs to be shored. I've got to get machinery in to put the shoring in.' 'Well, how long will that take?' 'About a couple of days.' 'Look, get the job done.' The JCB came in, dug the hole, the lad went down directing the pipes in, it caved in on top of him. Dead".

He explained:

---

325 Clauses 1(4) and 6

326 Clause 1(4)

327 Home Office, *Corporate Manslaughter: The Government's Draft Bill for Reform,* Cm 6497, March 2005, Explanatory Notes, para 12

328 Home Office, *Corporate Manslaughter: The Government's Draft Bill for Reform,* Cm 6497, March 2005, para 52

329 Volume II, Ev 11 and 210

330 Volume II, Ev 44, 88, 102,130,197,199,210, 247 and 250

331 Volume II, Ev 212

332 Volume II, Ev 11, 53, 65, 67, 83, 112, 127, 143, 172, 21, 234, 256, 263, 285, 295, 304 and 308 and Volume III, Q 17 [Ms Jones] and Q 316 [Mr Perks]

"the company went into court and pleaded guilty: 'Yes, we breached the Health and Safety at Work Act – fair cop, Guv' –and we killed the employee.' The judge was scathing on the company and then fined them £7,500. We think that is a scandal. I cannot justify that to the dependents or to the widow, that that is justice…Not only that, one of the directors put it to me in this way: 'Alan,' he said, 'one of your contracts has got £20,000 a day plus penalty clause for every day it is late. For us to introduce health and safety and to be rigid on it could possibly put that contract behind, whereas, if we break the Health and Safety at Work Act and kill the employee, we face an average fine of £7,000. It is a big choice for us as a company, isn't it?'. [333]

264. Witnesses argued that there was nothing in the proposals that would result in fines being imposed at a greater level than for current health and safety offences, unlimited fines being currently available for companies committed to the Crown Court for offences under the Health and Safety at Work etc. Act 1974.[334] Many therefore recommended that the Government should introduce a requirement or draft sentencing guideline that fines be commensurate with the seriousness of the offence, significantly higher than for convictions under the 1974 Act and linked to the profitability of the company.[335] They also argued that this would be fairer to smaller companies then receiving the same level of fine as a large company.[336] A level suggested by many was 10% of a company's annual turnover,[337] a figure that the Financial Services Authority can impose for financial mismanagement.

265. Other evidence suggested that before the sentencing process, courts should be given full information about the company, "including turnover, annual profits, history of relationship with the regulatory agency or its general health and safety record" in a report akin to social inquiry reports produced for individuals awaiting sentence.[338]

266. During the process of our inquiry Network Rail, formerly Railtrack, and Balfour Beatty were found guilty of breaching health and safety offences and given record sentences.[339] Network Rail was fined £3.5 million, a record for a rail firm on health and safety grounds, and the maintenance firm Balfour Beatty was fined £10 million. They were also ordered to pay £300,000 each in costs. However, union representatives believed that such levels of fines were exceptional and that fines for individual deaths in the workplace, rather than in very public disasters, would still remain low.[340] Professor Tombs from the Centre for Corporate Accountability also argued that the experience in other jurisdictions suggested that it was not sufficient to rely on judges to increase levels of fines:

---

333 Volume III, Q 343

334 Volume II, Ev 11, 83, 112, 127, 133, 134, 172, 197, 218, 223, 234, 256, 263, 285 and 295

335 Volume II, Ev 112, 143, 218, 223 and 285 and Volume III, Q 69[Mr Bergman]

336 Volume II, Ev 130

337 Volume II, Ev 83

338 Volume II, Ev 128

339 The court case followed the derailment in October 2000 of a London to Leeds train at Hatfield because of a broken rail. Four people died and 102 were injured in the incident.

340 Volume III, Q 30 [Mr Camfield]

"if we allow discretion for judges and rely upon judges to push up the fines for the bigger companies, actually beyond a certain level probably they will not do that. The evidence in the United States in the nineties, in fact, indicates that beyond a certain level judges simply will not go because the fines look absolutely outrageous, even though they may be a very small percentage of turnover".[341]

267. We note that some industry groups also called for sentencing guidelines. Case law has set out aggravating and mitigating features in relation to health and safety offences[342] and some of these organisations wanted clarity on whether these would be the criteria on which fines for corporate manslaughter would be based.[343]

268. **We welcome the higher sentences given in recent cases by courts following convictions for high profile health and safety offences which involved deaths. Nevertheless, the evidence suggests that there is a need for an improved system of fining companies. We recommend that, following the enactment of the Bill, the Sentencing Guidelines Council produce sentencing guidelines which state clearly that fines for corporate manslaughter should reflect the gravity of the offence and which set out levels of fines, possibly based on percentages of turnover. The Committee recognises that a term such as turnover would need to be adequately defined on the face of the Bill. It is particularly important that fines imposed for the corporate manslaughter offence are higher than those imposed for financial misdemeanours. We also believe that it would be useful for courts to receive a full pre-sentence report on a convicted company. This should include details of its financial status and past health and safety record.**

269. The Government's 2000 consultation document welcomed views on whether it would ever be appropriate for the prosecuting authority to institute proceedings to freeze company assets before criminal proceedings start in order to prevent them being transferred to evade fines or compensation orders. However, there was no mention of this in the draft Bill. Some witnesses expressed concern that if prosecuting authorities did not have this power, some guilty companies might avoid fines by shifting assets or going into liquidation.[344]

270. We discussed the possibility of freezing a company's assets in oral evidence with representatives of the Confederation of British Industry. They believed freezing the assets of a company under investigation "would be contrary to our concept of natural justice" as this would punish and possibly even ruin a company that might yet be found innocent.[345] However, they did float the idea of using "escrow accounts" as an alternative (albeit with many caveats).[346] This would involve putting the assets into the accounts of a third organisation until the outcome of an investigation and/or trial. **We believe that it is right**

---

341 Volume III, Q 69

342 *R v Howe* (1999) and *R v Friskies Petcare UK Limited* (2000)

343 See for example, Volume II, Ev 92.

344 Volume II, Ev 83, 127, 144 and 221

345 Volume III, Q 391 [Mr Roberts]

346 Volume III, Q 396 [Dr Asherson]

in principle that prosecuting authorities should have the power in appropriate cases to ensure that companies do not try to evade fines by shifting assets.

Remedial orders

271. The draft Bill also proposes that the courts be given the power to make orders requiring convicted organisations to remedy either (a) the gross breach of the duty of care; or (b) any matter resulting from it and appearing to have been a cause of the death.[347] Such an order would have to specify a period within which the required steps must be taken, which could be extended by application to the court.[348] Failure to comply with an order would be an offence punishable with an unlimited fine in the Crown Court or a fine of up to £20,000 in the magistrates' court.[349] Courts already have these powers under the Health and Safety at Work Act, but they appear never to have been used.[350]

272. Many witnesses welcomed the inclusion of remedial orders in the draft Bill.[351] They were seen to have a number of advantages, including offering the opportunity to ensure breaches did not reoccur;[352] and providing an alternative to a fine in cases of changed ownership between death and prosecution, where the error had not yet been resolved but, arguably, the new firm should not be penalised.[353]

273. Others expressed reservations about remedial orders. A frequently raised concern was that remedial orders would needlessly duplicate the existing powers of the Health and Safety Executive (HSE) and local authorities to require improvements.[354] Witnesses pointed out that the HSE and local authorities would be able to intervene much earlier, while remedial orders would presumably have to wait until a long investigation and complex Crown Court trial had led to conviction.[355] However, Mr Rees, Chief Executive of the HSE felt that there was still a case for giving courts remedial powers even if they were rarely used in practice. He told the Sub-committees:

> "it seems to me that there is a case for a remedial power but I think in practice, certainly for the territory covered by the Health and Safety at Work Act, I would be very surprised if it were used very greatly".[356]

274. Others also expressed concern that the Crown Prosecution Service and/or the courts would lack the safety management expertise needed to decide what remedial orders were appropriate.[357] Mr Adrian Lyons from the Railway Forum, for example, argued that:

---

347 Clause 6

348 Clause 6(2) and (3)

349 Clause 6(4)

350 Volume II, Ev 111

351 Volume II, Ev 43, 47, 67, 121 and 207

352 Volume II, Ev 71

353 Volume II, Ev 36

354 Volume II, Ev, 92, 111, 114, 128,152, 190 and 231

355 Volume II, Ev 144, 152 and 205

356 Volume III, Q 540

357 Volume II, Ev 64, 79, 93, 114, 128 191 and 338-339

"to leave it to a judge whose main focus is not on the safety process to make recommendations that could be binding on the industry would be particularly unsound in many cases".[358]

Yet JUSTICE believed that judges would rely on advice from the HSE when determining remedial orders.[359]

275. **We consider that remedial orders are unlikely to be frequently used in practice, as the Health and Safety Executive and local authorities are likely to have acted already. However, we believe they are an additional safeguarding power for cases where companies do not take appropriate action. We recommend that judges who do make use of this power should make full use of the expertise of the Health and Safety Executive and local authorities available to them.**

276. The evidence we received also made two suggestions about remedial orders. The first was that the draft Bill should include provision for an enforcement body to monitor and report on whether or not the organisation has complied with the remedy.[360] For example, Mr Christopher Donnellan of the Law Reform Committee of the General Council of the Bar argued;

"there needs to be clear identification of who is going to investigate that the compliance has been met".[361]

We believe this is a sensible suggestion. **We recommend that the Government considers mechanisms for monitoring whether an organisation, including a Crown one, has complied with a remedial order and includes a provision for this in the Bill.**

277. Second, Anne Jones from the Simon Jones Memorial Campaign argued that it should be possible to charge directors of a company with "contempt of court" when a company failed to follow the steps of a remedial order:

"I cannot see why, if the judge says, 'You have got to put everything right that causes death, you've got to increase staffing, improve training, improve communications, get the right machinery in place,' and so on, 'and you have got three months to do it,' if the company fails to do that then the directors are not in court on a 'contempt of court' charge, for which there is a custodial sentence. That might focus their minds on correcting the errors and omissions which caused the death in the first place".[362]

278. **We believe it is sensible to encourage directors of a company to take responsibility for ensuring their company complies with a remedial order. We therefore recommend that the Government amends the Bill in order to make it possible for directors to be charged with contempt of court if the company has failed to take the steps required by the court.**

358 Volume III, Q 211

359 Volume III, Q 486 [Ms Ireland]

360 Volume II, Ev 121 and 136

361 Volume III, Q 133

362 Volume III, Q 17 [Mrs Jones]

Application to Crown bodies

279. The draft Bill currently provides for Crown bodies convicted of the offence to be liable to fines and/or remedial orders.[363] In its introduction to the draft Bill, the Home Office invited comments on the argument that fining a Crown body served little practical purpose and was simply the recycling of public money through the Treasury and back to the relevant body to continue to provide services. Some organisations agreed with this argument.[364] Others pointed out that money might not pass back to a fined body and then the public services it delivered would suffer.[365] A number of witnesses also raised concerns that remedial orders would place the courts in the difficult position of telling the Government how to govern.[366]

280. However, a majority of the evidence submitted to us expressed the view that fines and remedial orders should apply to Crown bodies, arguing that this was important to ensure that justice was seen to be done.[367] The Institute of Directors, for example, wrote:

> "One problem that is being sought to be addressed by this legislation is the feeling that such a serious failing as causing death renders the perpetrator subject to nothing more than a slap on the wrist. It would be wrong if this were seen to be perpetuated for Crown bodies".[368]

281. Several witnesses argued that sanctioning Crown bodies would send out a powerful public message of culpability.[369] Some suggested that these sanctions could also lead to strengthening of accountability within a Government department[370] and that without such sanctions Crown bodies might not learn from their failures.[371] The Association of Train Operating Companies pointed out that fines could support remedial orders by being "targeted to the underlying systemic failures. For example restrictions could be made upon future budgets".[372] The Business Services Association argued that not having fines for Crown bodies would result in difficult questions as to whether groups made up of both private and public sector bodies could be fined and, if so, how fines should be distributed.[373]

282. **We believe that it is important that Crown bodies do not escape sanction and that fines and remedial orders can serve a practical purpose in signalling culpability.** However, some of the criticisms advanced against imposing fines and remedial orders

---

363 Clause 1(4) and 6

364 Home Office, *Corporate Manslaughter: The Government's Draft Bill for Reform*, Cm 6497, March 2005, para.53. See also Volume II, Ev 25, 43 137, 144, 222 and 234

365 Volume II, Ev 208, 304 and 312

366 Volume II, Ev 312

367 Volume II, Ev 76

368 Volume II, Ev 47

369 Volume II, Ev 42, 43, 121 and 297

370 Volume II, Ev 76, 121 and 228

371 Volume II, Ev 327

372 Volume II, Ev 92

373 Volume II, Ev 53

upon Crown bodies do have some validity. This strengthens our later argument that other sanctions should also be considered for this offence (see below).

Other sanctions

283. Some organisations did not agree that other sanctions were necessary, arguing that the damage done to a convicted company's reputation would be a deterrent in itself.[374] However, many witnesses believed the combination of fines and remedial orders would neither provide a sufficient deterrent against poor health and safety practices nor deliver justice.[375]

284. Many witnesses felt that an opportunity was being missed to introduce a wider and more innovative range of penalties.[376] Great disappointment was expressed that the Government had not taken the time in the eight years in which it had been planning this legislation to review alternatives. It was also pointed out that other jurisdictions imposed wider sanctions in similar laws.[377] For example, Mr David Bergman of the Centre for Corporate Accountability told the Sub-committees:

> "If the Government can be criticised for one thing, for which there is absolutely no excuse, it is the way it has dealt with sentences. It has had years to consider alternative ways of sentencing organisations and companies. Canadian provinces and Australian states have produced report after report after report detailing alternative forms of sentences that can be imposed upon organisations. They are out there, they are used, there are options available, and the fact that the British Government has not been able to do the sort of work that one small Canadian province or Australian state has been able to do in the last ten or 15 years is extraordinary. I just want to put that on the record".[378]

285. The Parliamentary Under-Secretary of State for the Home Office also told us that she welcomed "the fact that witnesses have suggested more innovative sanctions". She added that "it seems to me absolutely essential that we have a proper consultation process. I would be reluctant to delay the Bill in order to do that".[379] The Government has now established a review team in the Better Regulation Executive which amongst other things has been asked for views about ways of modernising the penalty regime in the regulatory system. Its review began in August 2005 and will run until September 2006. Its terms of reference include examining "whether alternative penalties, such as restitutive or restorative Orders, could be used as an alternative to fines in some cases".[380]

286. We believe that the key issue when determining whether alternative sanctions are needed in the draft Bill is whether those bereaved would find the suggested sanctions

---

374 Volume II, Ev 200, 241, 247, 252 and 266

375 Volume II, Ev 7, 17, 25 and 30

376 Volume II, Ev 7, 11, 25, 62, 133, 172, 190, 195, 263, 299, 308 and 322

377 Volume II, Ev 9 and 172

378 Volume III, Q 68

379 Volume III, Q 599

380 http://www.cabinetoffice.gov.uk/regulation/

meaningful. It is clear from the evidence we received that they do not. For example, Ms Pamela Dix of Disaster Action told us:

> "If I can deal briefly with the issue of fines in themselves, we think basically, on a philosophical basis, that they are meaningless…What is the point, except for a headline in a newspaper?…we would argue that it is not particularly meaningful either as punishment or deterrence".[381]

287. **We share the disappointment of many that the Government has not included more innovative corporate sanctions in the draft Bill. We welcome the fact that the Government is now looking at the issue of alternative penalties but believe that the scope of this review should be widened to look at alternative sanctions for non-regulatory offences. Remedial orders and fines provide an inadequate range of sanctions for sentencing. It is not clear, for example, if remedial steps already taken by an organisation will be taken into account in assessing the level of a fine. There clearly would be difficulties if fines made a company bankrupt if it had already taken successfully implemented remedial orders. We therefore think a wider range of sanctions is essential.**

288. Suggestions for alternative corporate sanctions presented to us in evidence included:

- company probation orders[382] or a corporate "death sentence" (i.e. mandatory dissolution);[383]

- naming and shaming organisations, through the Health and Safety Executive's Public Register of Conviction and/or publicity in the media, by notice or in the company's annual report;[384]

- confiscation of assets associated with the offending and prohibition of the corporation from business activities associated with the offending;[385]

- cessation from any activity in the company or company branch until an acceptable plan of action is introduced or the revocation of any relevant licence or statutory authorisation allowing the organisation to undertake its respective business activity;[386]

- equity fines;[387]

- punitive damages to be paid to relatives of victims.[388]

- the power to order the seizure of dangerous or defective equipment prior to conviction and the forfeiture and destruction of such equipment after conviction;[389]

---

381 Volume III, Q 16

382 Volume II, Ev 7, 11, 112, 133, 172, 207, 218, 222, 237 and 256

383 Volume II, Ev 11

384 Volume II, Ev 11, 26, 61,133, 172, 218, 237, 286 and 295

385 Volume II, Ev 11

386 Volume II, Ev 83 and 144

387 Volume II, Ev 11, 26, 172, 237 and 332

388 Volume II, Ev 26, 61, 112, 144, 192, 218 and 286

- restorative justice mechanisms;[390] and

- ensuring that conviction affects a company's Comprehensive Performance Assessment or leads to an Audit Commission inquiry.[391]

289. Witnesses also suggested that directors should face individual sanctions, including custodial sentences,[392] disqualification,[393] training orders;[394] and community service orders.[395] Since individual liability for directors is a key issue we deal with this separately in Chapter 13 below.

290. In our evidence gathering, we focused on three options for sanctioning companies in particular: equity fines, punitive damages and restorative justice.

Equity fines

291. Equity fines would require an organisation to create shares up to a particular value which would either be taken by the Government or go into a victims' fund. Amicus and Disaster Action felt that an advantage of such fines would be that they would reduce the value of shares in a company, which would be what companies feared most.[396] Mr Griffiths argued:

> "we think the chemistry between the management of the company, the investors represented by the shareholders and the workers in the company, to which management have a responsibility, is quite interestingly mixed by the application of an equity fine".[397]

Punitive damages

292. Some of the victims' groups that appeared before us criticised the levels of compensation currently available to victims. Ms Sophie Tarrasenko from Disaster Action argued that currently: "A death is very cheap if the person is over 18 and has no dependants and that is a glaring flaw in any system for us".[398] Mrs Eileen Dallaglio, who lost her daughter in the Marchioness disaster, told us:

> "the compensation took ten years to arrive… and it totalled £310.46".[399]

---

389 Volume II, Ev 144

390 Volume II, Ev 292

391 Volume II, Ev 207

392 Volume II, Ev 7, 11 and 112

393 Volume II, Ev 17, 26, 35, 133, 218 and 256

394 Volume II, Ev 26, 47, 172 and 256

395 Volume II, Ev 26, 47, 172 and 256

396 Volume II, Ev 234 and Volume III, Q 16 [Ms Tarrassenko]

397 Volume III, Q 48

398 Volume III, Q 16

399 Volume III, Q 319

78

293. Under section 130 of the Powers of Criminal Courts (Sentencing) Act 2000, criminal courts can award compensation following conviction for an offence. There was a conflict in evidence we received about the powers for awarding compensation under this Act. The Law Reform Committee of the General Council of the Bar stated, that the Act only applies to an offender who is an individual, so if the Government intended to make it possible for the Act to apply to an organisation, then the bill would need to clearly spell this out.[400] Ms Sally Ireland from JUSTICE, however, believed that the Act would already give courts the powers to order companies to make compensation.[401] **Irrespective of this dispute it is our view that the draft Bill should make provision for companies to be required to pay compensation.**

294. Most victims pursue damages through the civil courts. Some witnesses felt that the draft Bill should contain a provision allowing <u>punitive damages</u> to be awarded without recourse to civil action.[402]

295. However, other evidence warned against this proposal, arguing that "you are beginning to blur the boundaries between someone being sentenced for the offence and damages, which is a civil matter";[403] that criminal courts might not have the relevant expertise to set levels of damages;[404] and that the family would not be represented – only the prosecutor and the defendant.[405]

Restorative justice

296. The Restorative Justice Consortium pointed out that the Government had clearly stated that it intended to maximise the use of <u>restorative justice</u> in the Criminal Justice System and argued that corporate manslaughter was a "prime example" of the type of case where restorative justice would be "highly appropriate".[406] They suggested that "relatives and survivors should be offered the opportunity to meet senior managers …(or communicate with them indirectly if they did not wish to meet) so that they could ask questions, express their feelings and discuss the form, which any reparation or compensation should take".[407] In oral evidence, Mr Peter Schofield from EEF, the manufacturers' organisation, stated that his organisation had also considered the possibility of such a sanction.[408]

---

400 Volume II, Ev 122

401 Volume III, Q 489

402 Volume II, Ev 61, 127, 218 and 325, Volume III, Q 129 [Mr Antoniw]

403 Volume III, Q 129 [Mr Donnellan]

404 Volume III, Q 489[Ms Ireland]

405 Volume III, Q 489[Ms Ireland]

406 Volume II, Ev 291

407 Volume II, Ev 291

408 Volume III, Q 260

297. However, the Institution of Occupational Safety and Health argued that "[t]hough early evidence on the effects of re-offending seems encouraging, it is inconclusive, and there needs to be more research into its efficacy with respect to particular offences".[409]

298. We have not had the time in our oral evidence sessions, due to the tight Government timetable for pre-legislative scrutiny, to give full consideration to all the alternative sanctions suggested to us and we have therefore not taken a view about which of these sanctions would provide the best form of penalty. **We believe the Government should be aiming towards implementing a wide package of sanctions for corporate manslaughter, so that courts have the flexibility to match sanctions to the broad range of cases that might come before them.**

13 Individual liability for directors

299. Under the current common law offence of gross negligence manslaughter, individual officers of a company (directors or business owners) can be prosecuted for gross negligence manslaughter if their own grossly negligent behaviour causes death. This offence is punishable by a maximum of life imprisonment.[410] Between April 1999 and September 2005, 15 directors or business owners were personally convicted of this offence.

300. In addition, under the Health and Safety at Work etc. Act 1974, relevant officers of a company can be prosecuted for a health and safety offence which is committed by the company if that offence was the result of the officer's personal "consent", "connivance" or "neglect".[411] This health and safety offence is punishable with a fine[412] and directors who are found guilty can be disqualified from being a company director for up to two years.[413] Since 1986 only eight company directors have been disqualified on such grounds.

301. The Home Office has decided not to pursue new criminal sanctions against individuals in the draft Bill. It has also decided expressly to exclude secondary liability for individuals who would otherwise be guilty of aiding, abetting, counselling or procuring the offence of corporate manslaughter.[414] It justified this decision on the basis that "the need for reform arises from the law operating in a restricted way for holding organisations to account …and this is a matter of corporate not individual liability".[415] In oral evidence to the Sub-committees, the Parliamentary Under-Secretary of State at the Home Office, Fiona Mactaggart MP, argued that "the individual gross negligence manslaughter and the capacity to prosecute individuals under health and safety legislation do give one a framework where the individual level of responsibility can properly be dealt with".[416]

302. Our witnesses were divided on this issue. Half of the evidence we received agreed with the Government.[417] Representatives from industry argued that it would be wrong to include individual liability in the draft Bill. The British Vehicle Rental and Leasing Association, for example, submitted that:

> "those directors that are grossly negligent in their own right, of causing the death of a person to whom they owe a duty of care, can be prosecuted under the common law offence of manslaughter. It would be wholly inappropriate for the burden of proof or standard to be lowered simply to satisfy calls for a corporate scapegoat or because it may be challenging to prosecute the individual for his own actions or inactions…the Health and Safety at Work Act 1974 (HSWA) already acknowledges the principle of

---

410 Offences against the Person Act 1861, Section 5

411 Section 37(1)

412 Health and Safety at Work etc. Act 1974, section 37

413 Company Directors Disqualification Act 1986, section 2(1)

414 Clause 1(5)

415 Draft Corporate Manslaughter Bill, p 17

416 Volume III, Q 557

417 Volume II, Ev 14, 42, 43, 16, 40-50, 47, 54, 63, 78, 240-1, 92, 103, 113, 115, 190, 204, 210, 213, 252, 268, 271, 274, 295, 299 and 327

custodial sentences for individuals held responsible for the most serious omissions or acts."[418]

303. The Institute of Directors argued that:

"The change in the law is intended to close gaps in the application of that law, not to create a wider offence".[419]

304. Industry groups also raised concerns that provisions for individual liability under the corporate manslaughter offence might discourage managers from taking up posts directly managing risk or in high-risk industries.[420]

305. An eminent judge, Lord Justice Judge, also agreed with the Government's position and echoed industry concerns about individual liability. He told the Sub-committees in oral evidence that,

"We will have, assuming this becomes an Act, an offence of corporate manslaughter. You will not have abolished individual manslaughter, so individual responsibility will remain. I think that it would be very difficult to persuade anybody to take on the responsibility of senior manager within your definition if he were going to be liable to be found guilty for the inadequacy of the operation as a whole...'You will be the fall guy. You are the safety officer/manager or whatever it is. You are responsible for everything that goes wrong in the organisation.' I do not think anybody would do that job, because you are totally dependent on the quality of others, and those people not making mistakes..."[421]

306. However, many other witnesses to our inquiry argued that the lack of proposed punitive sanctions against individuals would provide an insufficient deterrent and would be unsatisfactory for those who wish to see justice delivered for the families of victims.[422] The Communication Workers' Union, for example, commented, "Ironically, Directors and Managers can be imprisoned for ..."Cooking The Books" but not for killing workers and members of the public".[423] Witnesses pointed out that the Government had agreed that individual liability would be necessary in its 2000 consultation paper[424] and that individual liability appeared to be supported in surveys by directors themselves.[425] It was also feared that if the proposed offence were introduced it might frustrate proceedings against individuals for manslaughter under the existing common law offence because prosecutors

---

418 Volume II, Ev 13

419 Volume II, Ev 45

420 Volume II, Ev 78, 53,103, 240, 338 and Volume III, Q 512 [Rt Hon Sir Igor Judge], Q 231 {Mr Commins] and Q 252 [Ms Peter]

421 Volume III, Q 517

422 Volume II, Ev 7, 11, 17, 26, 31, 43, 56, 60, 66, 79, 81, 190, 193, 222, 235, 262, 283, 298, 306, 314, 319, and 326, Volume III, Q 445 [Mr Stoddart]

423 Volume II, Ev 257

424 Volume II, Ev 7, 172 and 286

425 Volume II, Ev 11

might see companies as an easier target or because simultaneous proceedings might be seen as unfair for the individual.[426]

307. Witnesses suggested various ways of making directors or senior managers individually liable:

- Automatic liability whenever a company is found guilty of corporate manslaughter.[427]

- An additional offence of "unlawful killing" should be introduced, that would allow one or more directors and senior managers to be held individually responsible for workplace deaths if they are found to be responsible for the management failings leading to a corporate manslaughter conviction.[428]

- The offence of aiding, abetting, counselling or procuring an offence of corporate manslaughter should not be excluded in the draft bill.[429]

308. **We do not believe it would be fair to punish individuals in a company where their actions have not contributed to the offence of corporate manslaughter and we therefore reject the argument that individuals in a convicted company should be automatically liable. However, we believe that if the draft Bill were enacted as currently drafted there would be a gap in the law, where individuals in a company have contributed to the offence of corporate manslaughter but where there is not sufficient evidence to prove that they are guilty of individual gross negligence manslaughter.**

309. **The small number of directors successfully prosecuted for individual gross negligence manslaughter shows how difficult it is to prove the individual offence. Currently the only alternative would be to prosecute individuals for the less serious offence of being a secondary party to a health and safety offence. We believe that, just as the Government has taken the decision that when a company's gross management failing caused death it should be liable for a more serious offence than that available under health and safety legislation, so it should be possible to prosecute an individual who has been a secondary party to this gross management failing for a more serious offence also. We therefore recommend that secondary liability for corporate manslaughter should be included in the draft Bill.** (We believe that it would not be problematic to prosecute individuals for being a secondary party to a *corporate* offence – after all it is possible, under the current law for a woman to be a secondary party to rape.)

310. One way of achieving the inclusion of secondary liability would be simply to remove clause 1(5) of the Bill which expressly states that an "individual cannot be guilty of aiding, abetting, counselling or procuring an offence of corporate manslaughter". However, it would not be simple to convict an individual under this approach because the standard rules on participation in crime are not designed to deal with such activities. As Ms Sally Ireland from JUSTICE pointed out to us,

426 Volume II, Ev 314

427 Volume II, Ev 8 and 58

428 Volume II, Ev 61 and 133

429 Volume II, Ev 7, 11, 26, 61 and 144

"…It should be made clear that the standard concepts of accessorial liability in participating in the offence may not be appropriate here because the level of culpability required could be very low. It is one of the characteristics of this offence that it is made up of a chain of actions by a large number of people. What you do not want is somebody being labelled with a manslaughter conviction who objectively has only committed something of very low culpability. Having looked at the current law on accessorial liability on counselling and procuring, I think it should be necessary that the defendant intended that the offence or an offence of the same type should be committed. That is the law. That makes it quite difficult".[430]

311. The rules on participation in crime are currently being examined by the Law Commission which is scheduled to issue a consultation paper in 2006. This could lead to a change in the law with an unknown impact on the applicable rules in relation to corporate manslaughter.

312. A better alternative might therefore be to insert clauses into the draft Corporate Manslaughter Bill based on sections 36 and 37 in the Health and Safety at Work Act. This might take the following form:

"(1) Where an offence of corporate manslaughter is proved to have been committed with the consent or connivance of, or to have been attributable to any neglect on the part of, any director, manager, secretary or other similar officer of the organisation or a person who was purporting to act in such a capacity, he as well as the organisation shall be guilty of the offence of corporate manslaughter.

(2) Where the affairs of a body corporate are managed by its members, the preceding subsection shall apply in relation to the acts and defaults of a member in connection with his functions of management as if he were a director of the body corporate

(3) Where the commission by any person of corporate manslaughter is due to the act or default of some other person, that other person shall also be guilty of the offence, and a person may be charged with and convicted of the offence by virtue of this subsection whether or not proceedings are taken against the first-mentioned person"

This option was suggested to us by the London Criminal Courts Solicitors' Association.[431]

313. We note that the Government has accepted in other proposed legislation that it would be appropriate to prosecute directors and other company officers of a serious criminal corporate offence if it was committed with their consent or connivance. Clause 18 of the Terrorism Bill reads:

"18 Liability of company directors etc

(1) Where an offence under this Part is committed by a body corporate and is proved to have been committed with the consent or connivance of –

(a) a director, manager, secretary or other similar officer of the body corporate or,

430 Volume III, Q 473

431 Volume II, Ev 145-6

(b) a person who was purporting to act in that capacity,

he (as well as the body corporate) is guilty of that offence and shall be liable to be proceeding against and punished accordingly".

314. We believe that in cases where an individual has been found guilty of this secondary offence, they should be liable to the full range of sentences available. Consideration needs to be given to the maximum term of imprisonment for the offence. This would need to be less than the maximum available for gross negligence manslaughter (life imprisonment). **By analogy with the offence of causing death by dangerous driving the maximum term of imprisonment could be set at 14 years.** Further, in such cases we believe that it would be appropriate to bring disqualification proceedings against such convicted individuals.

Directors' duties

315. Currently directors have no positive obligations to ensure that their companies are complying with health and safety legislation. Some witnesses argued that the Bill should be used to introduce statutory health and safety duties on directors.[432] For example, the Fire Brigades Union argued:

> "These proposals are an essential part of any corporate manslaughter legislation if it is to be effective. They are not included in the draft Bill. This is a serious shortcoming."[433]

However, the Centre for Corporate Accountability, although supportive of such statutory duties, believed the Bill "was not the right vehicle for such a reform".[434]

316. In June 2000 the Government published its strategy for 'revitalising' health and safety.[435] One of the action points in this document was that the Health and Safety Commission would advise Ministers on how the law needed to be changed to make directors' responsibilities with respect to health and safety statutory.[436]

317. However, in its report into the work of the Health and Safety Commission and Executive the Work and Pensions Committee noted that the Government appeared to have changed its mind. The Committee recommended that the Government should "reconsider its decision not to legislate on directors' duties and that it bring forward proposals for pre-legislative scrutiny in the next Parliament".[437] In response the Government said that it had "asked HSC to undertake further evaluation to assess the

---

432 Volume II, Ev 7, 26, 83, 218, 325, 278, 264, 316 and 398

433 Volume II, Ev 217

434 Volume III, Ev 130

435 Department of the Environment, Transport and the Regions, *Revitalising Health and Safety: Strategy Statement*, June 2000

436 Department of the Environment, Transport and the Regions, *Revitalising Health and Safety: Strategy Statement*, June 2000, para 68

437 Work and Pensions Committee, Fourth Report of Session 2003-04, *The Work of the Health and Safety Commission and Executive*, HC 456-I, para 60

effectiveness and progress of the current measures in place, legislative and voluntary, and to report its findings and recommendations by December 2005".[438]

318. The Government's Companies Law Reform Bill introduced on 1 November 2005, introduces duties for directors but makes no mention of responsibilities for the management of health and safety in their company.

319. A recent review of published research commissioned by the Health and Safety Executive found that "the evidence available provides a strong, but not conclusive, basis for arguing that the imposition of 'positive' health and safety duties on directors would serve to usefully supplement the liability that they currently face under section 37 of the Health and Safety at Work Act".[439]

320. **We acknowledge that statutory health and safety duties could be introduced outside the Bill, but believe that since they might help clarify directors' duties with regard to corporate manslaughter law the Government should aim to introduce them either in the Bill, alongside the Bill, or as closely as possible afterwards.**

438 Work and Pensions Committee, Third Special Report of Session 2003-04, *Government Response to the Committee's Fourth Report into the Work of the Health and Safety Commission and Executive*, HC 1137, p 5

439 Philip James, Middlesex University Business School for the Health and Safety Executive, *Directors' Responsibilities for Health and Safety – A Peer Review of Three Key Pieces of Published Research*

14 Investigation and prosecution

Who should investigate and prosecute the offence?

321. The Government's 2000 consultation paper invited views on whether health and safety enforcing authorities in England and Wales should be given powers to investigate and prosecute the new offence, in addition to the police and Crown Prosecution Service. This suggestion has been dropped from the draft Bill on the basis that police involvement signalled "the position of the new offence as a serious offence under the general criminal law, rather than an offence that might be characterised as regulatory."[440] Many welcomed this decision.[441]

322. Some witnesses, however, believed that the Health and Safety Executive (HSE) and other enforcement agencies should be able to investigate and prosecute the offence. For example, the Law Reform Committee of the General Council of the Bar believed that there was no reason why this could not be done "in an appropriate case".[442]

323. We note, however, that the Association of Chief Police Officers had reservations about the HSE taking on an investigative role in a manslaughter case:

> "I think if we were to take the investigation of this offence away from the police then…that might be seen as perhaps watering down the seriousness of the offence and aligning it with health and safety breaches which, albeit serious offences in their own right, are not seen with the same stigma necessarily as homicide prosecutions."[443]

324. The Deputy Chief Executive of the HSE was also reluctant for the body to become involved in prosecuting the offence:

> "We would not want to be in the case of prosecuting manslaughter cases which are by their very nature much, much more complex and require a degree of specialism that we do not necessarily have."[444]

325. Moreover he suggested to us that the current arrangements between the investigatory bodies were working well:

> "At the moment if it is an issue of manslaughter, both under the existing law or individual manslaughter, we have the work related deaths protocol. The position is that the police would do the initial investigation and if they believed it was a manslaughter case they would continue the investigation, clearly working closely with us. If at some stage they decided it was not a manslaughter case then it would be

---

440 Home Office, *Corporate Manslaughter: The Government's Draft Bill for Reform,* Cm 6497, March 2005, para 58

441 Volume II, Ev 12, 44, 54, 89, 100 and 188

442 Volume II, Ev 121

443 Volume III, Q 438 (Detective Chief Constable Stoddart)

444 Volume III, Q 544 (Mr Rees)

transferred to us to deal with under Health and Safety at Work legislation and we would then take the prosecution."

326. A number of organisations did, however, believe that the police would require further training to investigate and prosecute the offence effectively.[445] Eversheds LLP argued:

"in our experience, there are still Police Forces whose experience of such investigations is extremely limited, and whose approach to investigations is not consistent."[446]

327. **We agree that the investigation and prosecution of corporate manslaughter should remain the responsibility of the police and Crown Prosecution Service. However, the Home Office should consider whether the police might need further training in investigating and prosecuting the offence.**

Investigatory powers

328. The new offence of corporate manslaughter will be listed as a serious arrestable offence under the Police and Criminal Evidence Act 1984 (PACE) and therefore police powers of investigation will be subject to that Act. Schedule 1 of PACE permits a circuit judge, on the application of a constable to authorise the police to enter premises and seize material where there is high level of urgency and where delay would have a deleterious impact on the investigation. The Association of Chief Police Officers (ACPO) submitted evidence to the inquiry that the current arrangements under PACE were insufficient for corporate manslaughter investigations:

"Access to this material may only be secured under an order granted by a judge (Schedule 1 PACE), rather than under warrant issued by a Justice of the Peace. This creates particular problems in obtaining an appropriate authority to access the business records of a company that is the subject of an investigation. By the time arrangements have been made to apply for such an order, and a hearing scheduled in front of a judge, the passage of time may have had a detrimental affect on the investigation".[447]

329. Under section 20 of the Health and Safety at Work etc. Act 1974, health and safety inspectors are provided with a number of powers for the purpose of carrying into effect enforcement responsibilities. These powers include powers of entry to premises, examination and investigation. Unlike the search and entry powers available for the police under PACE, Health and Safety Executive inspectors do not need to apply to a court for a warrant of authorisation. ACPO suggested that delays could be minimised by allowing a senior police to authorise warrants for entry and search rather than a circuit judge.

330. ACPO also requested additional powers to compel individuals to give evidence. They pointed out that individuals could not be cautioned as they were not liable to the offence and argued that witnesses against their own organisation were likely to be unwilling to help

445 Volume II, Ev 85, 170 and 241

446 Volume II, Ev 191

447 Volume II, Ev 323

the police. They stressed that the Serious Fraud Office and the Health and Safety Executive have powers to compel people to give evidence.[448] In addition they asked for powers to bring non-police expert support with them when necessary when entering business premises.

331. The Health and Safety Executive have expressed "some sympathy" with ACPO"s views "since it could avoid confusion and delay in some cases".[449]

332. However, JUSTICE was concerned about granting the police equivalent powers when investigating a serious criminal offence. It submitted:

> "The search of premises and seizure of documents can engage rights under both Article 6 (fair trial) and Article 8 (privacy) of the European Convention….[I]n these circumstances the need to apply an independent judicial authority in order to obtain a warrant is a necessary safeguard against the arbitrary use of powers of search and seizure. We therefore believe that the requirement for an application to a judicial authority should be maintained…".[450]

It suggested that there were other alternatives to extending powers to hasten the process, such as, for example, allowing a telephone hearing.[451]

333. The Centre for Corporate Accountability expressed support in principle for these new powers but questioned how they might work alongside different rules for evidence gathering in pursuit of an individual for gross negligence manslaughter.[452]

334. **We have yet to be convinced that the police require additional powers to investigate corporate manslaughter effectively. The requirement in the Police and Criminal Evidence Act 1984 to obtain judicial authority for entering and searching premises is an important safeguard. However, there does appear to be an inconsistency in the powers of the police and those of the Health and Safety Executive. We therefore urge the Government to consider this issue further.**

Consent to prosecute

335. Clause 1(5) of the draft Bill requires the consent of the Director of Public Prosecutions (DPP) before a private prosecution for a corporate manslaughter offence may be launched. This is a change of policy from the Government's 2000 consultation paper when there was no such requirement to obtain consent. In its introduction to the draft Bill the Government explains why this is no longer proposed:

> "There was significant concern amongst respondents that this would lead to insufficiently well-founded prosecutions, which would ultimately fail, and would

---

448 Volume II, Ev 324

449 Volume III, Ev 135

450 Volume III, Ev 135

451 Volume III, Ev 134

452 Volume III, Ev 129

place an unfair burden on the organisation involved with possible irreparable financial and personal harm".[453]

336. Some witnesses welcomed this decision.[454] For example, the British Retail Consortium argued:

> "We also welcome the intention that cases only be bought under the Crown Prosecution Service with the consent of the Director of Public Prosecutions as this should ensure that inappropriate cases are not brought under the legislation".[455]

337. A substantial number of witnesses however, strongly opposed this change in the proposals.[456] The Simon Jones Memorial Campaign disagreed that removing the requirement to obtain the consent of the DPP would lead to spurious and unfounded prosecutions:

> "Once more is it the interests of the potential offender that are put to the fore – not those of the victims and the bereaved families....The financial hurdles alone are so great that only in exceptional cases could a private prosecution be considered. There is therefore virtually no chance of an insufficiently well-founded private prosecution. For this reason alone it is unreasonable to add the additional obstacle of requiring the consent of the Director of Public Prosecutions".[457]

338. The Centre for Corporate Accountability quoted the Law Commission's original argument for not requiring the DPP's consent:

> "[T]he right of a private individual to bring criminal proceedings, subject to the usual controls, is in our view an important one which should not be lightly set aside. Indeed in a sense it is precisely the kind of case with which we are here concerned, where the public pressure for a prosecution is likely to be at its greatest, that that right is most important: it is in the most serious cases such as homicide, that a decision not to prosecute is most likely to be challenged. It would in our view be perverse to remove the right to bring a private prosecution in the very case where it is most likely to be invoked".[458]

339. It further added that "In any case, if a private prosecution is so manifestly unfounded, the case can be quickly quashed by the Crown court at an early stage".[459] The Centre also raised the concern that there could be some conflicts of interest in cases against the Crown.[460]

---

453 Home Office, *Corporate Manslaughter: The Government's Draft Bill for Reform,* Cm 6497, March 2005, para 60

454 Volume II, Ev 47, 77, 93, 104 109, 114, 268 and 271

455 Volume II, Ev 77

456 See, for example, Volume II, Ev 32, 60, 85, 114, 154, 253, 263, 268, 271, 290 and 302

457 Volume II, Ev 85

458 Quoted in Volume II, Ev 171

459 Volume II, Ev 171

460 Volume II, Ev 171

340. We consider that the interests of justice would be best served by removing the requirement to obtain consent. We are persuaded that this recommendation would not lead to spurious and unfounded prosecutions, as there exist a number of other obstacles to bringing a private prosecution for corporate manslaughter. **We recommend that the Government remove the provision in clause 1(4) requiring the Director of Public Prosecution's consent before a prosecution can be instituted.**

15 Cost

341. The Government argues that the proposed offence would not create any new regulatory burden and that major costs should only, therefore, be incurred by companies who currently fail to have adequate health and safety arrangements in place.[461] Its regulatory impact assessment does however, anticipate the following additional costs to industry and the state:

Costs to Industry:	
Defending the additional 5 prosecutions a year expected	£2.5 million
Legal advice on the new proposals	£6 million
Additional training costs	£6 million

Costs of prosecuting new offence	
Courts	£83,000
Crown Prosecution Service	£150,000

Total:	£14.7 million

342. The Government has pointed out that this total cost amounts to less than 0.1% of the costs incurred by the state, industry and individuals by work-related injuries, estimated at between £20 billion and £31.8 billion in 2001/02.[462] Accordingly, it argues, even a very small reduction in work-related deaths and injury would allow the costs to be met.[463]

343. However, we heard very mixed views on whether we should expect the number of deaths related to death and injury to reduce as a result of the enactment of this Bill. Mr Bill Callaghan, Chairman of the Health and Safety Commission suggested to us in oral evidence that we might see such a reduction "all other things being equal".[464]

344. However, CMS Cameron McKenna LLP believed the Government was making a "questionable" assumption. They argued:

"There is a notable dearth of evidence supporting the deterrent effect in individual offending generally, and in the health and safety sphere for companies in particular. We question whether deterrence can operate at all at the level of inadvertence and unconscious risk taking which is the typical characteristic of work place accidents. Claims about deterrent effect beg serious questions about the individual and

461 *Draft Corporate Manslaughter Bill*, para 30

462 *Draft Corporate Manslaughter Bill*, para 26

463 *Draft Corporate Manslaughter Bill*, para 55

464 Volume III, Q 525

collective behaviour of individuals in large organisations. There seems to be a confusion here with the issue of pursuing 'compliance' strategies, which are conceptually quite distinct from deterrence and form part of complex regulatory structures (like that of the HSWA). Even more questionable is how there can be a 'marginal deterrent' effect from an offence which carries the same unlimited maximum fine as a serious health and safety offence . Certainly no evidence has been put forward to help understand how such an effect would work, or what other (less desirable) consequences might also arise".[465]

345. The Government's regulatory impact assessment also made the following further points related to cost:

- the five additional prosecutions expected annually should not be treated as entirely new since health and safety charges would be likely to have been bought in such cases;[466]

- the offence would have a beneficial impact on small and medium enterprises (SMEs) by creating a "level playing field" by making it easier to prosecute larger companies for corporate manslaughter;[467] and

- there would be no additional costs of investigation to the Health and Safety Executive(HSE) or the police as the HSE already investigate work-related deaths and major public incidents are already subject to full police investigation.[468]

346. Some witnesses agreed with the Government and did not anticipate large additional costs.[469]

347. However, many did consider that the proposals would have significant cost implications.[470] Some believed there would be an increase in spurious claims if the Bill were enacted costing companies money in defending themselves.[471] The Confederation of British Industry, for example, commented:

"[t]he expectation by the Home Office, that the offence will attract no more than five prosecutions a year, is a heroic assumption. There is a significant possibility that pressure groups will seek to press for prosecution in a much larger number of cases…it will be tempting for enforcers to put forward corporate manslaughter papers to the CPS rather than justify inaction and poor usage of the new law to a sceptical section of the public".[472]

465 Volume II, Ev 102

466 *Draft Corporate Manslaughter Bill,* para 39

467 *Draft Corporate Manslaughter Bill,* paras 46 and 47

468 *Draft Corporate Manslaughter Bill,* para 39

469 Volume II, Ev 8, 48, 226 and 301

470 Volume II, Ev 199, 301, and 305

471 Volume II, Ev 1, 54, 63, 78, 79, 189, 210 and 253

472 Volume II, Ev 249

348. The Crime Committee of the Police Superintendents' Association believed the Bill would result in protracted and resource-intensive police investigations.[473] Others argued that the Bill would put pressure on companies to move towards formally certified Health and Safety Management systems with additional costs.[474] It was also feared that the Bill could discourage foreign investment.[475]

349. Some industry groups also warned that the Bill might encourage "risk averse" behaviour which would result in some costs.[476] The Railway Forum, for example, warned that "the prevalence of a 'safety at any price' approach in many areas has had serious consequences, particularly with regard to industry performance and cost".[477] However, the Centre for Corporate Accountability dismissed such arguments. Mr Bergman, Director of the Centre, argued, "[W]e are very sceptical of a lot of rhetoric about risk-averse conduct and the way that is being used to try to question the merits of the Bill, because clearly an offence of this kind will, we hope, deter inappropriate risk-averse conduct that goes on at the moment".[478] The Railway Forum also pointed out to us that "[R]isk aversion is an outcome of confusion, to be blunt, people not understanding what they are meant to be doing or felling disorientated".[479]

350. EEF, the manufacturers' organisation warned that some consultants might try to captialise on such misunderstanding and "unscrupulously exploit the passing of the legislation in order to generate business to convey false messages about what actually is required".[480] We also heard evidence that the Bill would in fact have a disproportionate impact on SMEs since they would have less resources to consider the new offence and might be more likely to rely on such consultancy. Dr Janet Asherson from the Confederation of British Industry argued, "[T]hey may overreact and pay more, comparative to their profit base or to their running costs".[481]

351. The Local Authorities Co-ordinators of Regulatory Services pointed out that local authorities are co-enforcers of the Health and Safety at Work Act along with the HSE. They therefore felt the Government's regulatory impact assessment should have considered the costs to local authorities even if they were neutral.[482]

352. **We did not receive substantial evidence to suggest that companies that currently have adequate health and safety arrangements in place would incur major costs when complying with this legislation. We recommend that the Government works with industry advisory bodies to try to educate industry about the offence and therefore minimise the cost of legal advice and training.**

473 Volume II, Ev 39

474 Volume II, Ev 37, 53, 54, 63,78, 241, 249 and 272

475 Volume II, Ev 210 and 249

476 Volume II, Ev 40, 77 and 87

477 Volume II, Ev 40

478 Volume III, Q 51

479 Volume III, Q 184 [Mr Lyons]

480 Volume III, Q 276 [Mr Schofield]

481 Volume II,I Q 364

482 Volume II, Ev 66

Conclusions and recommendations

1. We welcome the Government's proposal to introduce a statutory offence of corporate manslaughter. (Paragraph 16)

2. We are concerned at the length of time it has taken the Government to introduce a draft Bill since it first promised legislation on corporate manslaughter. We believe there should be no further unnecessary delay. We urge the Government to introduce the Bill, including our recommended changes, by the end of the present parliamentary session, making provision for carry-over if necessary. (Paragraph 49)

3. As the Government's proposals stand, it will be possible to prosecute corporations under the provisions in the draft Bill, and individuals running smaller unincorporated bodies will be able to be prosecuted under the common law individual offence of gross negligence manslaughter. However, a gap in the law will remain for large unincorporated bodies such as big partnerships of accounting and law firms. We are concerned that such major organisations will be outside the scope of the Bill and would recommend that the Government look at a way in which they could be brought within its scope. We urge the Government to provide us with statistics in order to support its claim that the inability to prosecute large unincorporated bodies does not cause problems in practice. We would be particularly interested in seeing statistics detailing how many large unincorporated bodies have been prosecuted and convicted of health and safety offences. (Paragraph 62)

4. We welcome the certainty provided by an exhaustive list of government departments and other bodies and believe that the alternative, providing a statutory definition, could prove very difficult if not impossible to achieve. We agree with the Home Office that the draft Schedule needs "further work" to ensure that a number of other bodies, including a range of executive agencies, are included. It should also be reviewed by the Home Office on an ongoing basis, and formally every six months to ensure it is up to date. We think it might also be useful to extend clause 7 to ensure that bodies which are successors to bodies included in the Schedule are treated as "organisations" to which the offence applies. (Paragraph 65)

5. We recommend that the Home Secretary's delegated power to amend the Schedule should be subject to the affirmative resolution procedure rather than the negative resolution procedure. (Paragraph 67)

6. It is appropriate that police forces as well as police authorities should be subject to the proposed new offence. We welcome the Government's assurances that the Bill when introduced will contain such provision. (Paragraph 71)

7. We welcome the Government's proposal that the offence not be limited only to the deaths of workers. (Paragraph 74)

8. We believe that organisations should be punished where their failings cause serious injury but are not convinced that gross negligence resulting in serious injury needs to be brought within the scope of the draft Bill. If the draft Bill was amended in this

way, it might lose its current clear focus on manslaughter, and the ensuing controversy and drafting difficulties might further delay the introduction of the actual Bill. We would, however, urge the Government to consider the possibility of using the Corporate Manslaughter Act as a template for introducing further criminal offences, such as an offence of corporate grievous bodily harm, in due course. (Paragraph 81)

9.	We are satisfied that the Bill as currently drafted covers long-term fatal damage to health as well as deaths caused by immediate injury. However, we would urge the Government to ensure that sufficient resources are available and appropriate procedures in place to make certain that in practice prosecutions are brought for deaths related to occupational health causes. (Paragraph 84)

10.	We are satisfied that the title of the offence should be "Corporate Manslaughter" not "Corporate Killing". (Paragraph 88)

11.	We recommend that the Government provide certainty on the law of causation, as it applies to corporate manslaughter, by including the Law Commission's original clause in the Bill. (Paragraph 94)

12.	We propose that the Home Office should remove the concept of 'duty of care in negligence' from the draft Bill and return to the Law Commission's original proposal that the offence should not be limited by reference to any existing legal duties but that an organisation should be liable for the offence whenever a management failure of the organisation kills an employee or any other person affected by the organisation's activities. We also recommend that whether an organisation has failed to comply with any relevant health and safety legislation should be an important factor for the jury in assessing whether there has been a gross management failure. Organisations are already required to comply with duties imposed under such legislation and so should already be familiar with them. (Paragraph 105)

13.	If the Government does decide to continue to base the offence on duties of care owed in negligence we do not believe the common law concept concerned should be limited by introducing categories where a duty of care must be owed. We are particularly concerned that the material accompanying the draft Bill did not highlight the use of the word "supply" and its intended purpose of automatically excluding certain activities "provided" by the state. (Paragraph 108)

14.	We agree that it should be possible to prosecute parent companies when a gross management failure in that company has caused death in one of their subsidiaries. (Paragraph 113)

15.	We are concerned by the suggestion that it may not be possible to prosecute parent companies under the current law, as courts have not ruled that parent companies have a duty of care in relation to the activities of their subsidiaries. This is an additional argument in favour of our recommendation that the offence should not be based on civil law duties of care. (Paragraph 115)

16.	We believe that, where a death of an agency worker or of an individual in a sub-contracting company was caused by a gross management failure by an employment agency or main contractor, it should be possible to prosecute these organisations jointly to establish either collective or individual corporate liability. We urge the Government to ensure that the Bill provides for this. (Paragraph 119)

17. We believe that principal contractors and employment agencies should take responsibility for the health and safety conditions of their sub-contractors and workers but that it is a step too far to provide that they should always be liable when a death has occurred. Principal contactors and employment agencies should only be liable when their own management failure is at fault. Anything more than this might encourage sub-contracting companies and those employing agency workers to ignore their health and safety responsibilities. (Paragraph 122)

18. We are very concerned that the senior manager test would have the perverse effect of encouraging organisations to reduce the priority given to health and safety. (Paragraph 136)

19. We agree that the offence does appear simply to broaden the identification doctrine into some form of aggregation of the conduct of senior managers. This is a fundamental weakness in the draft Bill as it currently stands. By focusing on failures by individuals within a company in this way, the draft Bill would do little to address the problems that have plagued the current common law offence. (Paragraph 140)

20. We are greatly concerned that the senior manager test will introduce additional legal argument about who is and who is not a "senior manager". (Paragraph 149)

21. We believe that the Government should be aiming for an offence that applies equitably to small and large companies. (Paragraph 154)

22. We note that the reference to senior managers might also have the unfortunate effect of discouraging unpaid volunteers from taking on such roles. (Paragraph 158)

23. We recommend that the Home Office reconsiders the underlying "senior manager" test. (Paragraph 159)

24. We believe that a test should be devised that captures the essence of corporate culpability. In doing this, we believe that the offence should not be based on the culpability of any individual at whatever level in the organisation but should be based on the concept of a "management failure", related to either an absence of correct process or an unacceptably low level of monitoring or application of a management process. (Paragraph 169)

25. We appreciate the reason for limiting the application of the offence to gross breaches, if utilising a concept of duty of care. This targets this serious criminal offence at the gravest management failures. (Paragraph 172)

26. We welcome the general proposal to include in the draft Bill an indicative, not exhaustive, list of factors which jurors are required to consider when determining whether an organisation's conduct is a gross breach. However, given the levels of apparent confusion, we would urge the Government to provide a clear explanation of how such a list of factors would be used in court. (Paragraph 179)

27.   We welcome the proposal in clause 3 of the draft Bill that the jury be required to have regard to whether the organisation has failed to comply with relevant health and safety legislation and guidance and that they be required to consider how serious was the failure to comply. This is an appropriate factor for juries to consider when determining whether there has been a gross management failure. We further recommend that after "legislation," the phrase "or any relevant legislation" be inserted in order to widen the scope of this factor. (Paragraph 187)

28.   We recommend that juries should not be required to consider a factor which makes reference to senior managers in an organisation. However, if this factor is retained, we believe it should refer to the "risk of death" only and not the "risk of death or serious harm" as this would be inconsistent with the current law of gross negligence manslaughter. (Paragraph 191)

29.   We are not convinced that the question of whether senior managers sought to cause the organisation to profit or benefit from the failure is relevant to determining whether there has been a gross breach. We therefore recommend that Clause 3(2)(b)(iii) be deleted. This factor should, however, be considered in sentencing. (Paragraph 194)

30.   We urge the Government to consider returning to the Law Commission's original proposal as a starting point. We acknowledge the argument that the Law Commission's "management failure" test could cover failings within a company that occur at too low a level to be fairly associated with the company as a whole. Nevertheless, we recommend that the Home Office should address this specific concern without abandoning the Law Commission's general approach. We suggest that juries be assisted in their task by being required to consider whether there has been a serious breach of health and safety legislation and guidance or other relevant legislation. In assessing this they could consider whether a corporate culture existed in the organisation that encouraged, tolerated or led to that management failure. (Paragraph 199)

31.   We welcome the proposal to remove Crown immunity for the offence of corporate manslaughter. However, we consider that the force of this historic development is substantially weakened by some of the broad exemptions included in the draft Bill. (Paragraph 204)

32.   We also note that five years have passed since the Government committed itself to removing Crown immunity for health and safety offences. We urge the Government to legislate on this issue as soon as possible. (Paragraph 205)

33.   The definition of "exclusively public function" is unsatisfactory. If the Government does decide to retain this exemption, the definition would need further work to ensure that there is clarity about the situations in which it would apply. (Paragraph 213)

34.   We are very concerned by the exemption for exclusively public functions and are not convinced by the Government's arguments for including in the Bill a blanket exemption for deaths resulting from the exercise of public functions. We do not consider that there should be a general exception under this heading since bodies

exercising such public functions will still have to satisfy the high threshold of gross breach before a prosecution can take place, namely that the failure must be one that "falls far below what could be reasonably expected." We do not consider that a private or a Crown body should be immune from prosecution where it did not meet this standard and as a result, a death occurred. (Paragraph 217)

35. We believe that there is no principled justification for excluding deaths in prisons or police custody from the ambit of the offence. The existence of other accountability mechanisms should not exclude the possibility of a prosecution for corporate manslaughter. Indeed public confidence in such mechanisms might suffer were it to do so. We are particularly concerned that private companies running prisons or custody suites, which are arguably less accountable at present, would be exempt. Accordingly, we recommend that, where deaths in prisons and police custody occur, they should be properly investigated and the relevant bodies held accountable before the courts where appropriate for an offence of corporate manslaughter. (Paragraph 227)

36. We believe that there should be an exemption to the offence for public policy decisions. However, we believe that this should only apply at a high level of public policy decision-making. (Paragraph 233)

37. Although we recognise the unique position of the armed forces, we consider that the exemption is drawn too widely. We are concerned that "preparation" for combat operations would encompass routine training and believe that such a wide exemption cannot be justified. We therefore recommend that the words "in preparation for" be removed from clause 10(1)(a) so that the exemption is restricted to combat operations and acts directly related to such operations. (Paragraph 239)

38. We are concerned by the possibility that the inclusion of police and fire operational activities might lead to a culture of risk averseness. However, this could be countered by effective education. We believe that the Bill should be drafted so that emergency services' operational activities are only liable for the offence in cases of the gravest management failings. (Paragraph 245)

39. We recommend that the offence be extended so that deaths that take place in the rest of the UK are within the scope of the offence when the management failure occurred in England and Wales. We also urge the Government to make provision in the Bill for the offence later to be extended at least to cover cases where deaths have occurred in the rest of the European Union. Although we understand that evidential and jurisdictional factors mitigate against the offence applying to UK bodies operating elsewhere in the world, we consider that the Government should take to itself a power to require information from the relevant UK body about such a death. (Paragraph 254)

40. Although we accept that it will be inevitable that there are some differences between the law on corporate manslaughter or culpable homicide in England and Wales and in Scotland because of the difference in the two legal regimes, the Government should be doing all it can to ensure there is as little practical variation as possible. We

note that the recommendations in our report would bring the Government's draft Bill closer to the reforms proposed by the Scottish Expert Group. (Paragraph 259)

41. We welcome the higher sentences given in recent cases by courts following convictions for high profile health and safety offences which involved deaths. Nevertheless, the evidence suggests that there is a need for an improved system of fining companies. We recommend that, following the enactment of the Bill, the Sentencing Guidelines Council produce sentencing guidelines which state clearly that fines for corporate manslaughter should reflect the gravity of the offence and which set out levels of fines, possibly based on percentages of turnover. The Committee recognises that a term such as turnover would need to be adequately defined o n the face of the Bill. It is particularly important that fines imposed for the corporate manslaughter offence are higher than those imposed for financial misdemeanours. We also believe that it would be useful for courts to receive a full pre-sentence report on a convicted company. This should include details of its financial status and past health and safety record. (Paragraph 268)

42. We believe that it is right in principle that prosecuting authorities should have the power in appropriate cases to ensure that companies do not try to evade fines by shifting assets. (Paragraph 270)

43. We consider that remedial orders are unlikely to be frequently used in practice, as the Health and Safety Executive and local authorities are likely to have acted already. However, we believe they are an additional safeguarding power for cases where companies do not take appropriate action. We recommend that judges who do make use of this power should make full use of the expertise of the Health and Safety Executive and local authorities available to them. (Paragraph 275)

44. We recommend that the Government considers mechanisms for monitoring whether an organisation, including a Crown one, has complied with a remedial order and includes a provision for this in the Bill. (Paragraph 276)

45. We believe it is sensible to encourage directors of a company to take responsibility for ensuring their company complies with a remedial order. We therefore recommend that the Government amends the Bill in order to make it possible for directors to be charged with contempt of court if the company has failed to take the steps required by the court. (Paragraph 278)

46. We believe that it is important that Crown bodies do not escape sanction and that fines and remedial orders can serve a practical purpose in signalling culpability. (Paragraph 282)

47. We share the disappointment of many that the Government has not included more innovative corporate sanctions in the draft Bill. We welcome the fact that the Government is now looking at the issue of alternative penalties but believe that the scope of this review should be widened to look at alternative sanctions for non-regulatory offences. Remedial orders and fines provide an inadequate range of sanctions for sentencing. It is not clear, for example, if remedial steps already taken by an organisation will be taken into account in assessing the level of a fine. There clearly would be difficulties if fines made a company bankrupt if it had already taken

successfully implemented remedial orders. We therefore think a wider range of sanctions is essential. (Paragraph 287)

48.   Irrespective of this dispute it is our view that the draft Bill should make provision for companies to be required to pay compensation. (Paragraph 293)

49.   We believe the Government should be aiming towards implementing a wide package of sanctions for corporate manslaughter, so that courts have the flexibility to match sanctions to the broad range of cases that might come before them. (Paragraph 298)

50.   We do not believe it would be fair to punish individuals in a company where their actions have not contributed to the offence of corporate manslaughter and we therefore reject the argument that individuals in a convicted company should be automatically liable. However, we believe that if the draft Bill were enacted as currently drafted there would be a gap in the law, where individuals in a company have contributed to the offence of corporate manslaughter but where there is not sufficient evidence to prove that they are guilty of individual gross negligence manslaughter. (Paragraph 308)

51.   The small number of directors successfully prosecuted for individual gross negligence manslaughter shows how difficult it is to prove the individual offence. Currently the only alternative would be to prosecute individuals for the less serious offence of being a secondary party to a health and safety offence. We believe that, just as the Government has taken the decision that when a company's gross management failing caused death it should be liable for a more serious offence than that available under health and safety legislation, so it should be possible to prosecute an individual who has been a secondary party to this gross management failing for a more serious offence also. We therefore recommend that secondary liability for corporate manslaughter should be included in the draft Bill. (Paragraph 309)

52.   By analogy with the offence of causing death by dangerous driving the maximum term of imprisonment could be set at 14 years. (Paragraph 314)

53.   We acknowledge that statutory health and safety duties could be introduced outside the Bill, but believe that since they might help clarify directors' duties with regard to corporate manslaughter law the Government should aim to introduce them either in the Bill, alongside the Bill, or as closely as possible afterwards. (Paragraph 320)

54.   We agree that the investigation and prosecution of corporate manslaughter should remain the responsibility of the police and Crown Prosecution Service. However, the Home Office should consider whether the police might need further training in investigating and prosecuting the offence. (Paragraph 327)

55.   We have yet to be convinced that the police require additional powers to investigate corporate manslaughter effectively. The requirement in the Police and Criminal Evidence Act 1984 to obtain judicial authority for entering and searching premises is an important safeguard. However, there does appear to be an inconsistency in the powers of the police and those of the Health and Safety Executive. We therefore urge the Government to consider this issue further. (Paragraph 334)

56. We recommend that the Government remove the provision in clause 1(4) requiring the Director of Public Prosecution's consent before a prosecution can be instituted. (Paragraph 340)

57. We did not receive much substantial evidence to suggest that companies that currently have adequate health and safety arrangements in place would incur major costs when complying with this legislation. We recommend that the Government works with industry advisory bodies to try to educate industry about the offence and therefore minimise the cost of legal advice and training. (Paragraph 352)

Annex 1 – Table showing development of current policy

Policy issue	Law Commission 1996 Paper	Government Consultation Paper 2000	Draft Bill
Who the Bill applies to	Any corporation, however and wherever incorporated (so including abroad), other than a corporation sole, but not unincorporated bodies or individuals, even as a second party.	All forms of undertaking, including partnerships, schools, unincorporated charities and small businesses; also parent and other groups companies if it could be shown that their own management failures were a cause of the death concerned.	Corporations, but not unincorporated bodies; also parent corporations (as well as any subsidiary) if a gross management failure by their senior managers caused death
Application to the Crown	No comment	Welcomed views on the application of Crown immunity to the offence of corporate killing.	Removal of Crown immunity with exemptions.
Causation	Separate provision, to the effect that management failure may be regarded as a cause of a person's death notwithstanding that the immediate cause is the act or omission of an individual.	Separate provision, to the effect that management failure may be regarded as a cause of a person's death notwithstanding that the immediate cause is the act or omission of an individual.	No separate provision. The Home Office argue that case law in this area has developed since the Law Commission reported and that no separate provision is now needed.
Management Failings	Defined as failures in the way an organisation's activities are managed or organised.	Defined as failures in the way an organisation's activities are managed or organised.	Defined as failures in the way an organisation's activities are managed or organised by an organisation's *senior managers*.
Corporate Behaviour Caught (Gross Breach)	Conduct that falls far below what can reasonably be expected in the circumstances.	Conduct that falls far below what can reasonably be expected in the circumstances.	Conduct that falls far below what can reasonably be expected in the circumstances, with a range of factors for assessing a company's culpability.
Relevant Duty of Care	Ensuring the health and safety of employees or members of the public. No definition of the	Ensuring the health and safety of employees or members of the public. No definition of the	That owed under the law of negligence by an organisation: as employer or occupier of land

	relationship between this and duties imposed by health and safety legislation and duties imposed under the common law to take reasonable care for the safety of others.	relationship between this and duties imposed by health and safety legislation and duties imposed under the common law to take reasonable care for the safety of others.	when supplying goods or services or when engaged in other commercial activities (for example, in mining or fishing). other than when carrying out exclusively public functions. The draft bill also exempts decisions involving matters of public policy.
Sanctions	Fines and powers to courts to give remedial orders.	Fines and powers to courts to give remedial orders, plus individual sanctions (see below).	Fines and powers to courts to give remedial orders.
Territorial Application	Liability for the corporate offence only if the injury that results in death is sustained in such a place that the English courts would have had jurisdiction over the offence had it been committed by an individual other than a British subject.	Liability for the corporate offence only if the injury that results in death is sustained in such a place that the English courts would have had jurisdiction over the offence had it been committed by an individual other than a British subject.	Liability for the corporate offence only if the injury that results in death is sustained in such a place that the English courts would have had jurisdiction over the offence had it been committed by an individual other than a British subject.
Individual Liability for Directors	None, apart from through existing health & safety law & individual manslaughter law.	Any individual who could be shown to have had some influence on, or responsibility for, the circumstances in which a management failure falling far below what could reasonably be expected was a cause of a person's death should be subject to a disqualification from acting in a management role in any undertaking carrying on a business or activity in Great Britain; also invited views on whether officers of undertakings if they contribute to the management failure resulting in death, should be liable to a penalty of imprisonment in separate criminal proceedings.	No new sanctions or plans to pursue secondary liability for individuals.

Private prosecutions	No consent from the Director of Public Prosecutions required	No consent from the Director of Public Prosecutions required	Consent of the Director of Public Prosecutions required before proceedings for the new offence can be instituted.
Powers to investigate and prosecute	No comment	The health and safety enforcing authorities and possibly other enforcement agencies should investigate and prosecute the new offences, in addition to the police and CPS; also invited views on whether it would ever be appropriate to permit the prosecuting authority to institute proceedings to freeze company assets before criminal proceedings start to prevent assets being transferred to evade fines or compensation orders.	The current responsibilities of the police to investigate and the CPS to prosecute corporate manslaughter will not change. The Home Office argues that the police and CPS already work jointly with the HSE and a protocol for liaison between agencies has been developed.

Formal minutes

Monday 12 December 2005

**The Draft Corporate Manslaughter Bill Sub-committee of the Home Affairs
Committee and the Draft Corporate Manslaughter Bill Sub-committee of the Work
and Pensions Committee met concurrently, in accordance with the provisions of
Standing Order No. 137A (Select committees: power to work with other committees).**

Members present:

Home Affairs Draft Corporate Manslaughter Bill Sub-Committee	*Work and Pensions Draft Corporate Manslaughter Bill Sub-Committee*
Mr James Clappison	Harry Cohen
Mrs Ann Cryer	Mr Philip Dunne
Mrs Janet Dean	Mrs Natascha Engel
Gwyn Prosser	Justine Greening
	Mr Terry Rooney

Mr Terry Rooney was called to the Chair, in accordance with the provisions of Standing
Order No. 137A (1)(d) (Select committees: power to work with other committees).

Report text

The Sub-committees considered this matter, in accordance with the provisions of Standing
Order No. 137A(1)(b).

Mr John Denham took the Chair.

Report text

The Sub-committees continued to consider this matter.

WORK AND PENSIONS DRAFT CORPORATE MANSLAUGHTER BILL SUB-COMMITTEE

The Home Affairs Draft Corporate Manslaughter Bill Sub-committee withdrew.

Mr Terry Rooney, in the Chair.

Harry Cohen	Mrs Natascha Engel
Mr Philip Dunne	Justine Greening

Consideration of report by Work and Pensions Draft Corporate Manslaughter Bill Sub-committee

Draft Report [*Draft Corporate Manslaughter Bill*], proposed by the Chairman, brought up and read.

Ordered, That the draft Report be read a second time, paragraph by paragraph.

Paragraphs 1 to 307 read and agreed to.

Paragraphs 308 to 314 read.

Amendment proposed, to leave out paragraphs 308 to 314 and insert the following new paragraph:

'**We do not believe it would be fair to punish individuals in a company where their actions have not contributed to the offence of corporate manslaughter and we therefore reject the argument that individuals in a convicted company should be automatically liable. We also do not believe there is a need for any form of secondary liability in the draft Bill. If the draft Bill is enacted, individuals will continue to be liable for individual gross negligent manslaughter, an offence punishable by a maximum of life imprisonment, where they are individually responsible for a death. Where they have consented or connived to or where their neglect has led to a health and safety offence they can also be individually prosecuted under sections 36 and 37 of the Health and Safety at Work etc. Act 1974, an offence punishable with a fine and that can lead to disqualification. We believe it would be inappropriate and unfair to introduce an additional form of liability. Such a route would also have the unfortunate effect of discouraging individuals from taking up posts directly managing risk or in high-risk industries. We therefore agree with the approach the Government has taken on this issue.**'

-(*Mr Philip Dunne*)

Question put, That the Amendment be made.

The Committee divided.

Ayes, 2	Noes, 2
Mr Philip Dunne	Harry Cohen
Justine Greening	Mrs Natascha Engel

Whereupon the Chairman declared himself with the Noes.

Paragraphs 308 to 314 agreed to.

Paragraphs 315 to 352 read and agreed to.

Annex agreed to.

Resolved, That the Report be the First Report of the Sub-Committee to the Committee.

Ordered, That the Chairman do make the Report to the Committee.

Ordered, That the Appendices to the Minutes of Evidence taken before the Sub-committees, be reported to the Committee.

[The Sub-committee adjourned.

HOME AFFAIRS DRAFT CORPORATE MANSLAUGHTER BILL SUB-COMMITTEE

The Work and Pensions Draft Corporate Manslaughter Bill Sub-committee withdrew.

Mr John Denham, in the Chair

Mr James Clappison	Gwyn Prosser
Mrs Janet Dean	

Consideration of Report by Home Affairs Draft Corporate Manslaughter Bill Sub-committee

Draft Report [*Draft Corporate Manslaughter Bill*], proposed by the Chairman, brought up and read.

Ordered, That the draft Report be read a second time, paragraph by paragraph.

Paragraphs 1 to 307 read and agreed to.

Paragraphs 308 to 314 read.

Amendment proposed, to leave out paragraphs 308 to 314 and insert the following new paragraph:

'**We do not believe it would be fair to punish individuals in a company where their actions have not contributed to the offence of corporate manslaughter and we therefore reject the argument that individuals in a convicted company should be automatically liable. We also do not believe there is a need for any form of secondary liability in the draft Bill. If the draft Bill is enacted, individuals will continue to be liable for individual gross negligent manslaughter, an offence punishable by a maximum of life imprisonment, where they are individually responsible for a death. Where they have consented or connived to or where their neglect has led to a health and safety offence they can also be individually prosecuted under sections 36 and 37 of the Health and Safety at Work etc. Act 1974, an offence punishable with a fine and that can lead to disqualification. We believe it would be inappropriate and unfair to introduce an additional form of liability. Such a route would also have the unfortunate effect of discouraging individuals from taking up posts directly managing risk or in high-risk industries. We therefore agree with the approach the Government has taken on this issue.**'

-(*Mr James Clappison*)

Question put, That the Amendment be made.

108

The Committee divided.

Ayes, 1   Noes, 2

Mr James Clappison   Mrs Janet Dean
                                           Gwyn Prosser

Paragraphs 308 to 314 agreed to.

Paragraphs 315 to 352 read and agreed to.

Annex agreed to.

Resolved, That the Report be the First Report of the Sub-Committee to the Committee

Ordered, That the Chairman do make the Report to the Committee.

Ordered, That the Appendices to the Minutes of Evidence taken before the Sub-committees, be reported to the Committee.

[The Sub-committee adjourned.

FURTHER PROCEEDINGS OF THE HOME AFFAIRS AND WORK AND PENSIONS COMMITTEES RELATING TO THE REPORT

The Home Affairs and Work and Pensions Committees met concurrently, in accordance with the provisions of Standing Order No. 137A (Select committees: power to work with other committees).

Members present:

Home Affairs Committee	*Work and Pensions Committee*
Mr James Clappison	Harry Cohen
Mrs Janet Dean	Mr Philip Dunne
Mr John Denham	Mrs Natascha Engel
Gwyn Prosser	Justine Greening
	Mr Terry Rooney

Mr John Denham was called to the Chair, in accordance with the provisions of Standing Order No. 137A (1)(d) (Select committees: power to work with other committees).

Consideration of report by concurrent committees

Draft report from Draft Corporate Manslaughter Bill Sub-committees [Draft Corporate Manslaughter Bill] brought up and read.

Ordered, That the Chairman's draft report be considered concurrently, in accordance with the provisions of Standing Order No. 137A (1)(c).

Ordered, That the draft Report be read a second time, paragraph by paragraph.

Paragraphs 1 to 352 read and agreed to.

Annex agreed to.

WORK AND PENSIONS COMMITTEE

The Home Affairs Committee withdrew.

Mr Terry Rooney, in the Chair

Harry Cohen   Mrs Natascha Engel
Mr Philip Dunne   Justine Greening

Consideration of report by Work and Pensions Committee

Resolved, That the Report [*Draft Corporate Manslaughter Bill*] be the First Report of the Committee to the House.

Ordered, That the Chairman do make the Report to the House.

Ordered, That the Appendices to the Minutes of Evidence taken before the Sub-committees be reported to the House.

Ordered, That the Report be published as a joint report, in accordance with the provisions of Standing Order No. 137A (2)

Ordered, That embargoed copies of the Report be made available, in accordance with the provisions of Standing Order No. 134.

[Adjourned till Wednesday 14 December at a quarter-past Nine o'clock.

HOME AFFAIRS COMMITTEE

The Work and Pensions Committee withdrew.

Mr John Denham, in the Chair

Mr James Clappison   Gwyn Prosser
Mrs Janet Dean

Consideration of report by Home Affairs Committee

Resolved, That the Report [*Draft Corporate Manslaughter Bill*] be the First Report of the Committee to the House.

Ordered, That the Chairman do make the Report to the House.

Ordered, That the Appendices to the Minutes of Evidence taken before the Sub-committee be reported to the House.

Ordered, That the Report be published as a joint report, in accordance with the provisions of Standing Order No. 137A (2)

Ordered, That embargoed copies of the Report be made available, in accordance with the provisions of Standing Order No. 134.

[Adjourned till tomorrow at Ten o'clock.

RELEVANT PARTS OF MINUTES OF PROCEEDINGS OF DRAFT CORPORATE MANSLAUGHTER BILL SUB-COMMITTEES RELATING TO DECLARATIONS OF INTEREST

MONDAY 24 OCTOBER

Mr Philip Dunne declared a pecuniary interest during the evidence session as the holder of directorships.[483]

THURSDAY 10 NOVEMBER

Harry Cohen declared a non-pecuniary interest as a member of the Union of Construction Allied Trades and Technicians Parliamentary Panel.

---

483 Mr Philip Dunne declared the following directorships to the Work and Pensions Committee on 19 July 2005: Baronsmead VCT – 4 – PLC, Non Executive Director, Venture Capital Trust and Ottakar's plc, Non Executive Director and Chairman, Retail Bookseller; remunerated employment - Gatley Farms, partner, farming partnership and Ruffer LLP, designated Member and Non Executive Representative on its Management Board, Investment Managers

List of witnesses

List of written evidence

Additional written evidence submitted to the Sub-committees published in Volume III

List of written evidence

Written evidence published in Volume II

116

Printed in the United Kingdom by The Stationery Office Limited
12/2005   324418   19585

2/9. ⁄

27/8

10/9

11/9 .

3/9 ⁄

28/8

26/8

7/9. Tort .

1/9 .

24/8

4ᵗʰ. September

ISBN 0-215-02668-3

9 780215 026682